Margaret Of Athens

The One Only Collection

By

Margaret Simmons

Margaret Of Athens

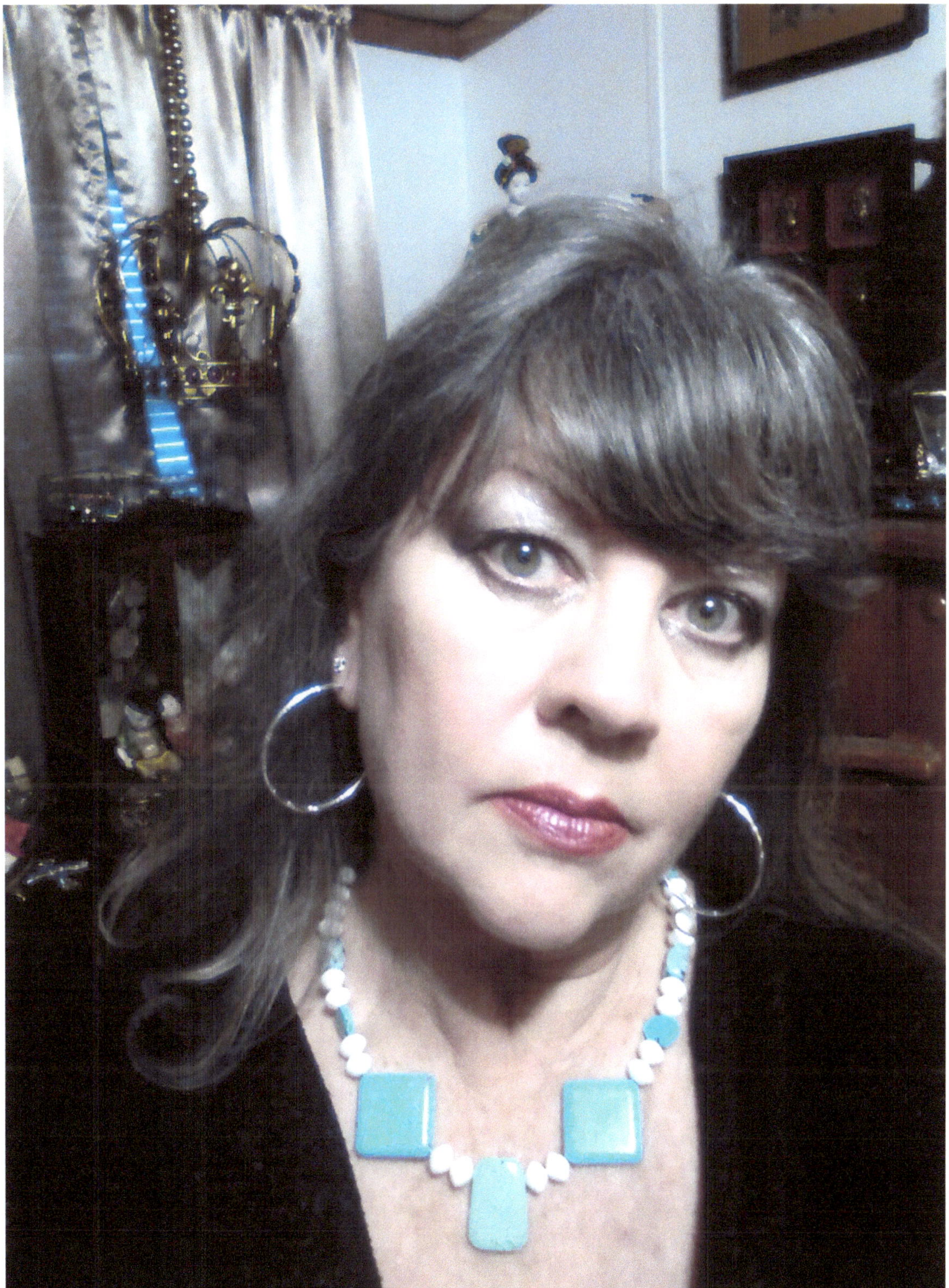

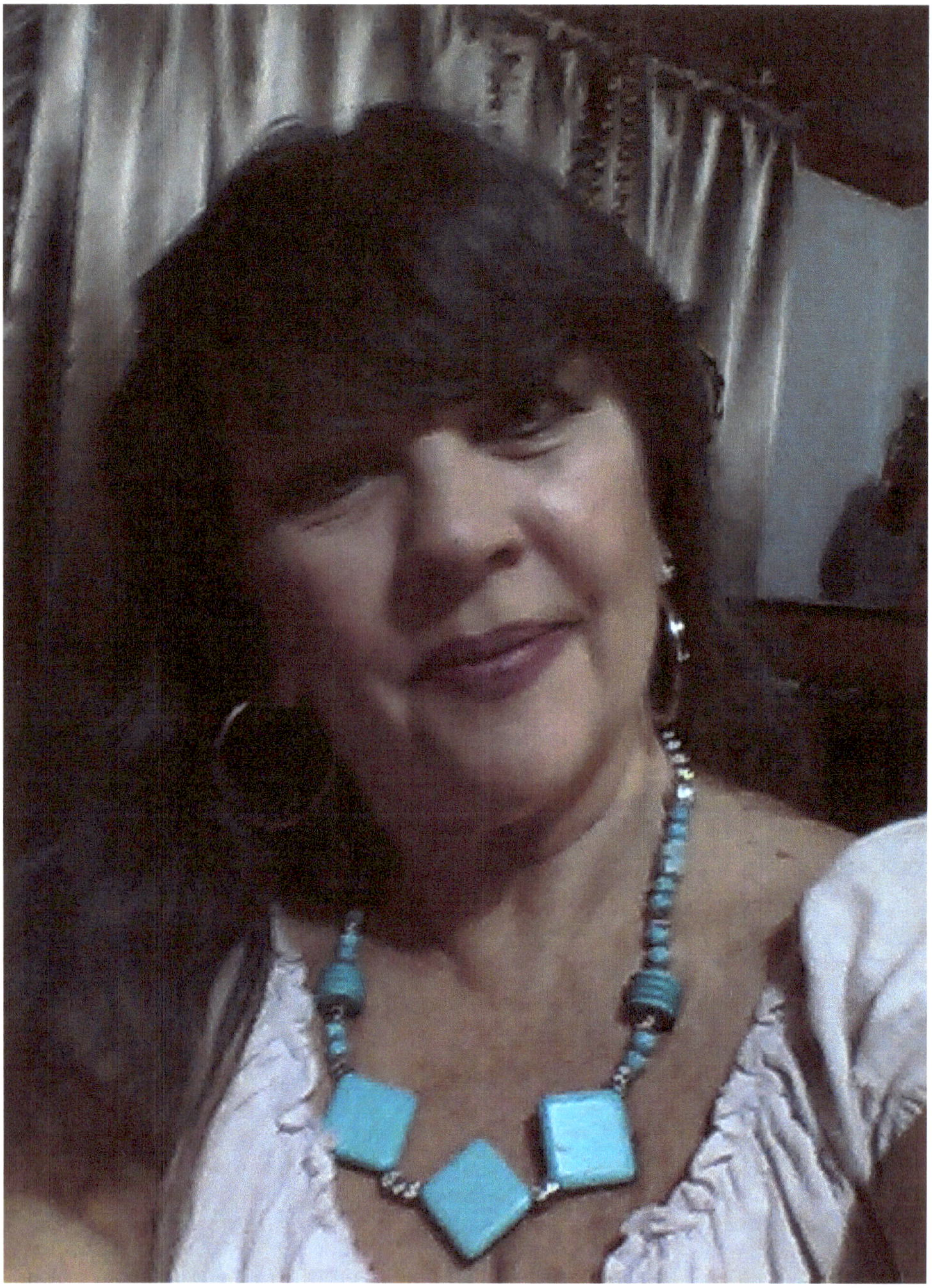

Margaret Of Athens

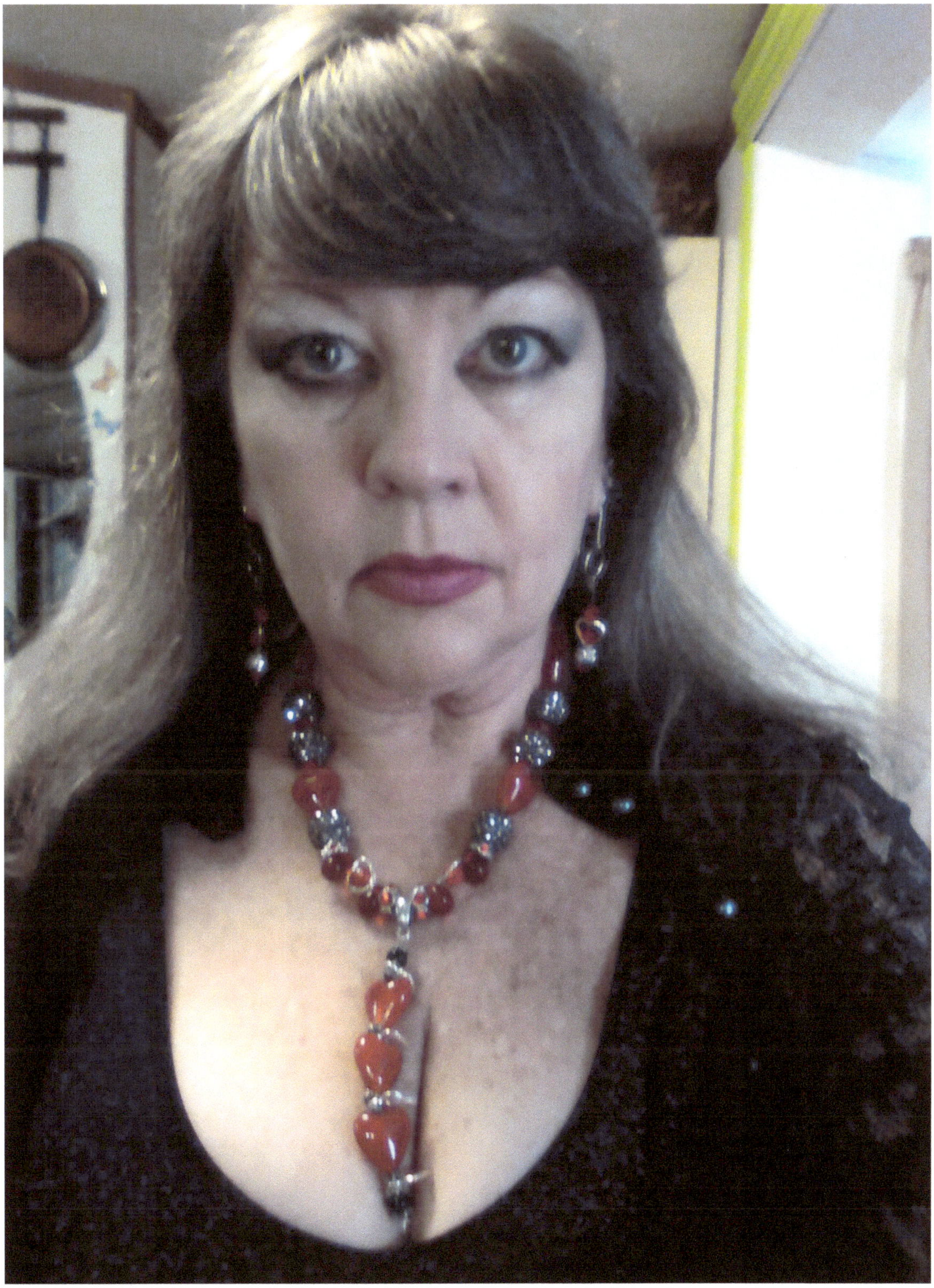

Margaret Of Athens

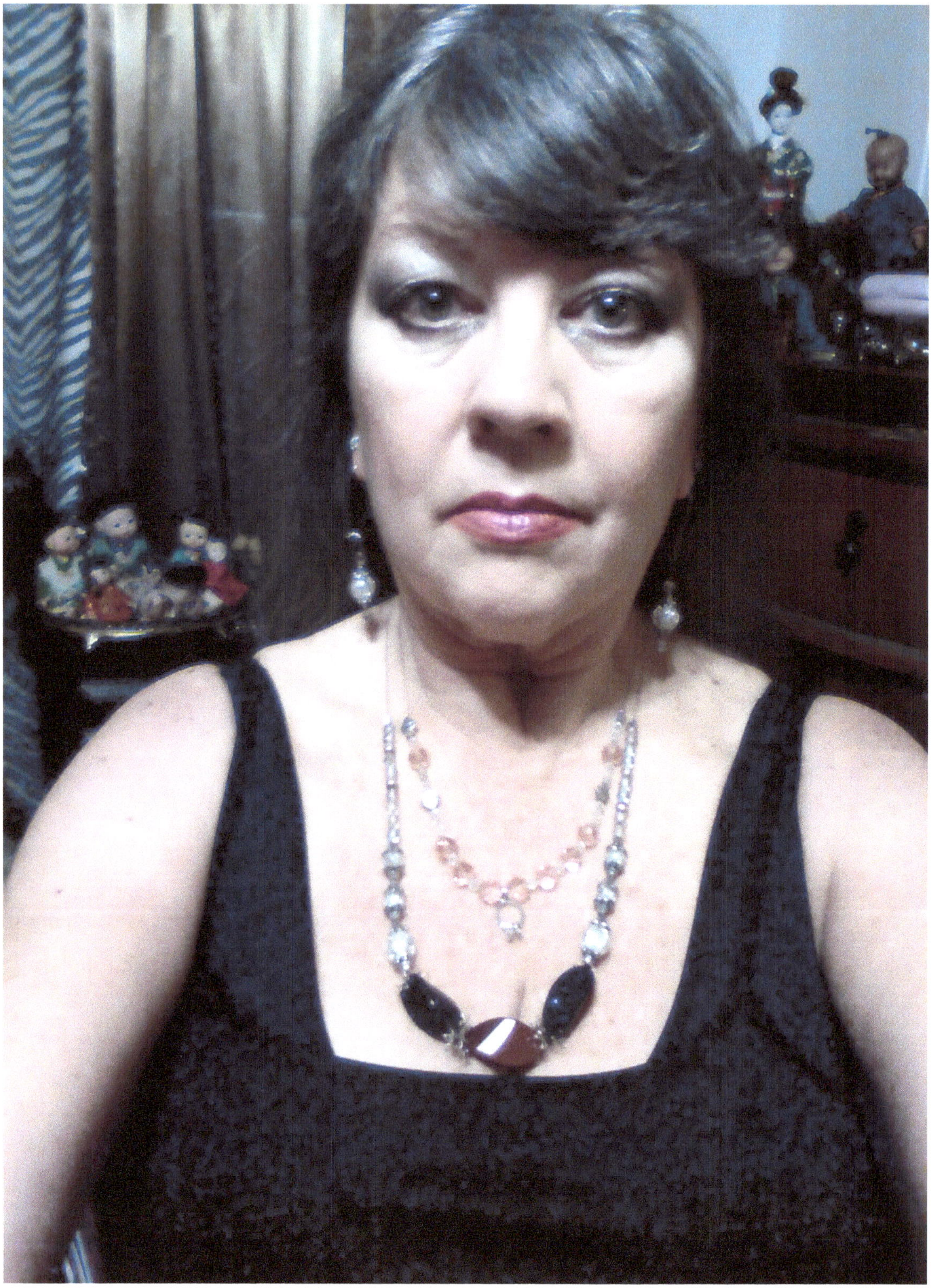

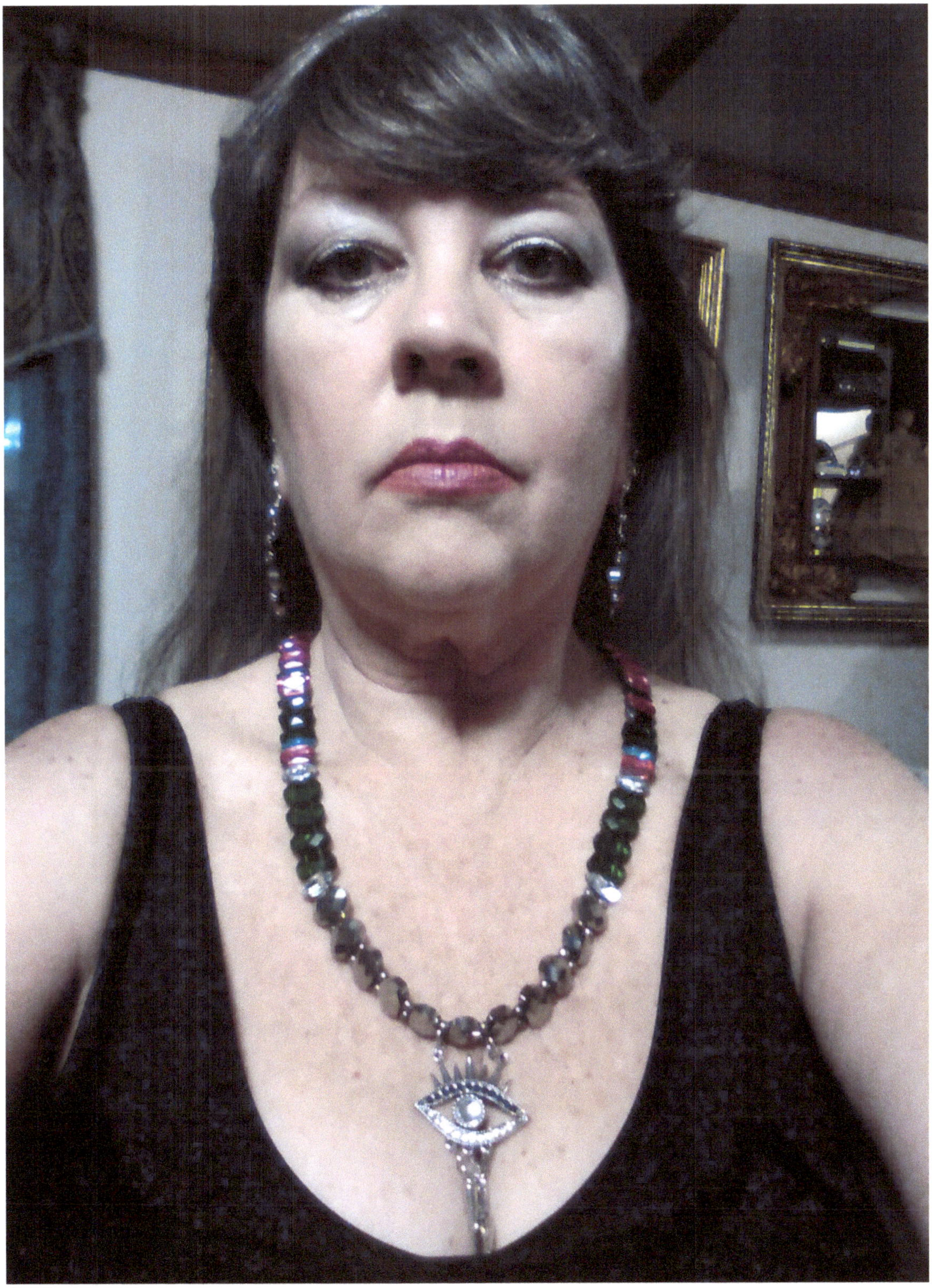

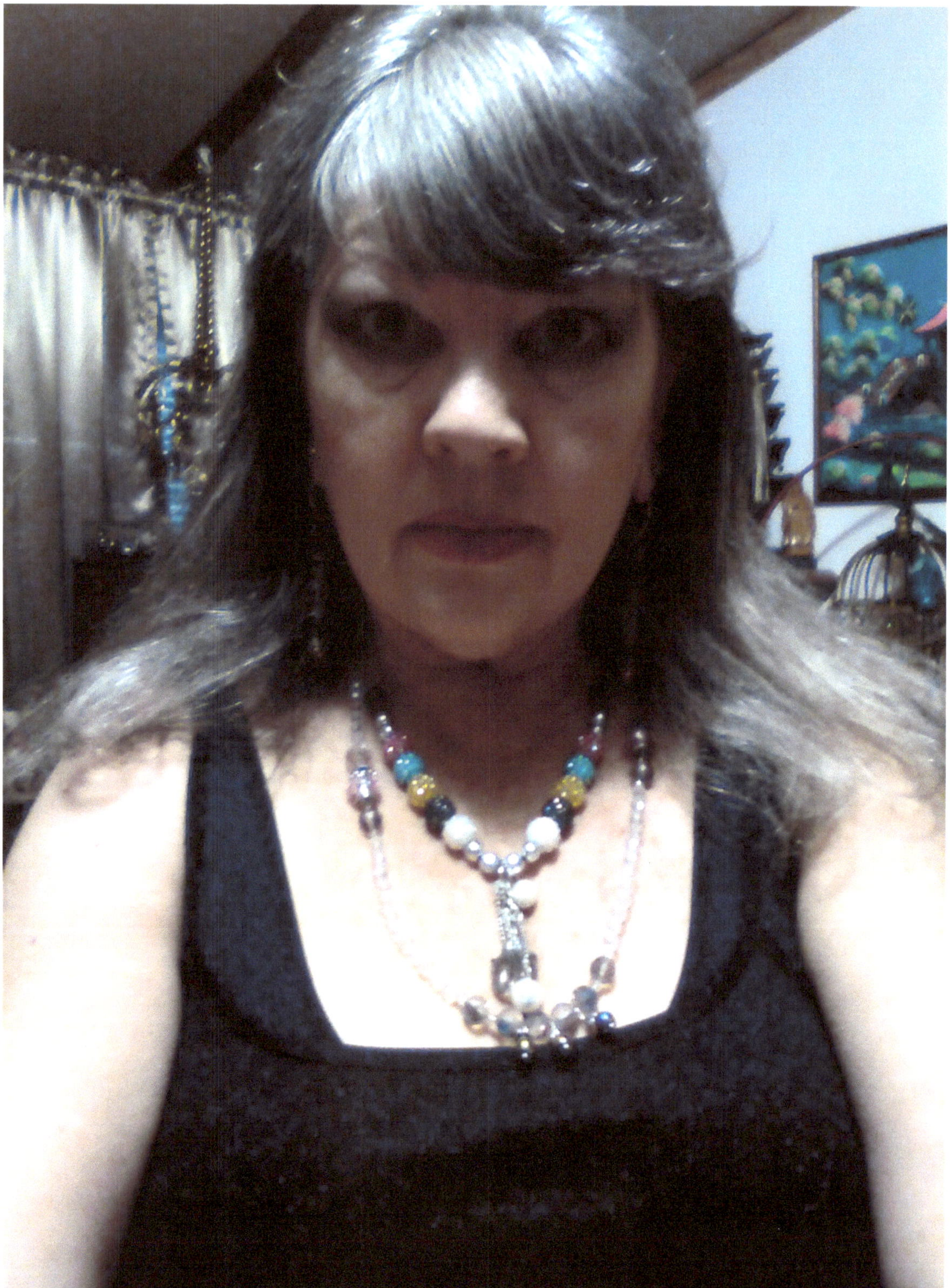

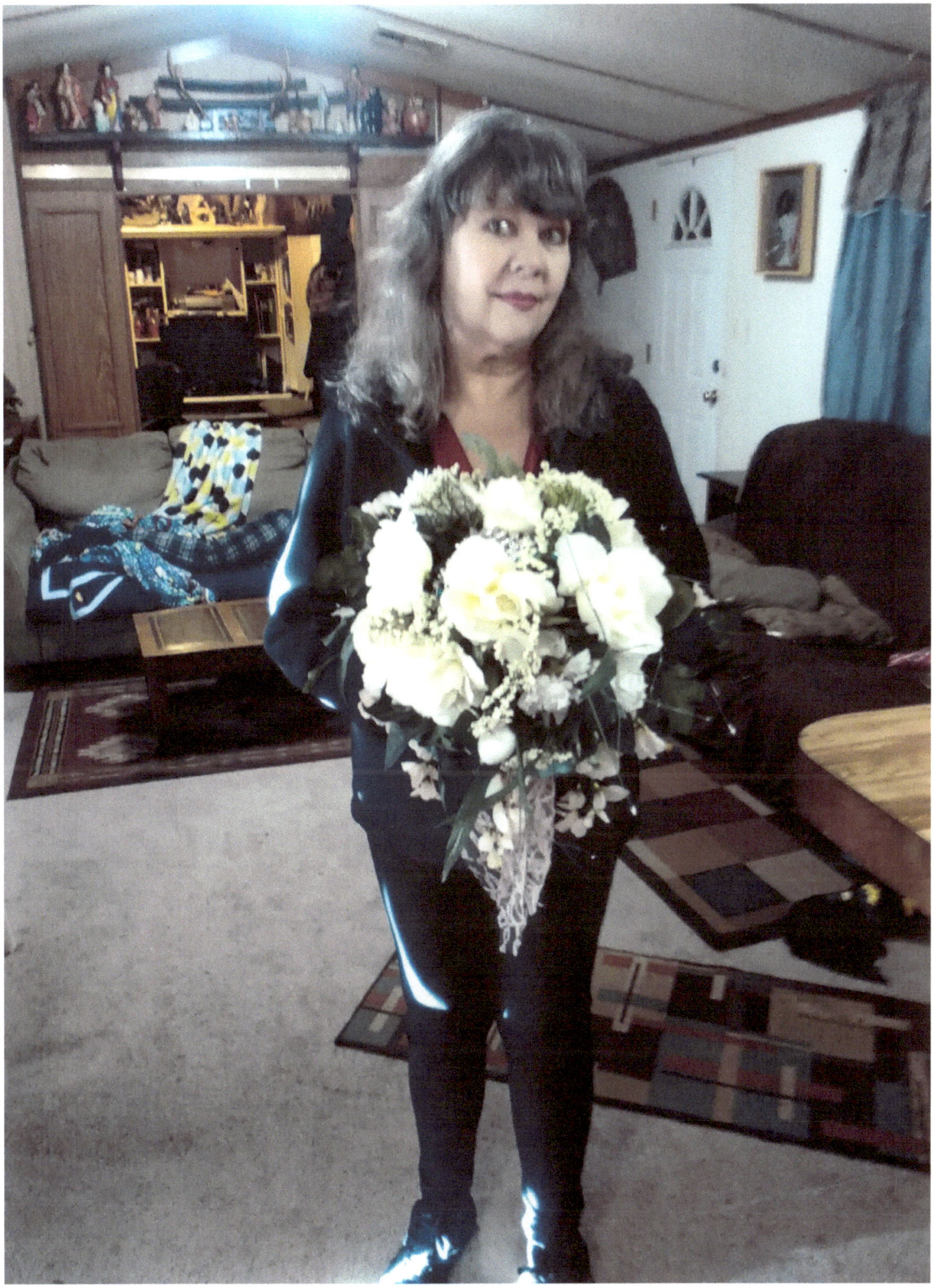

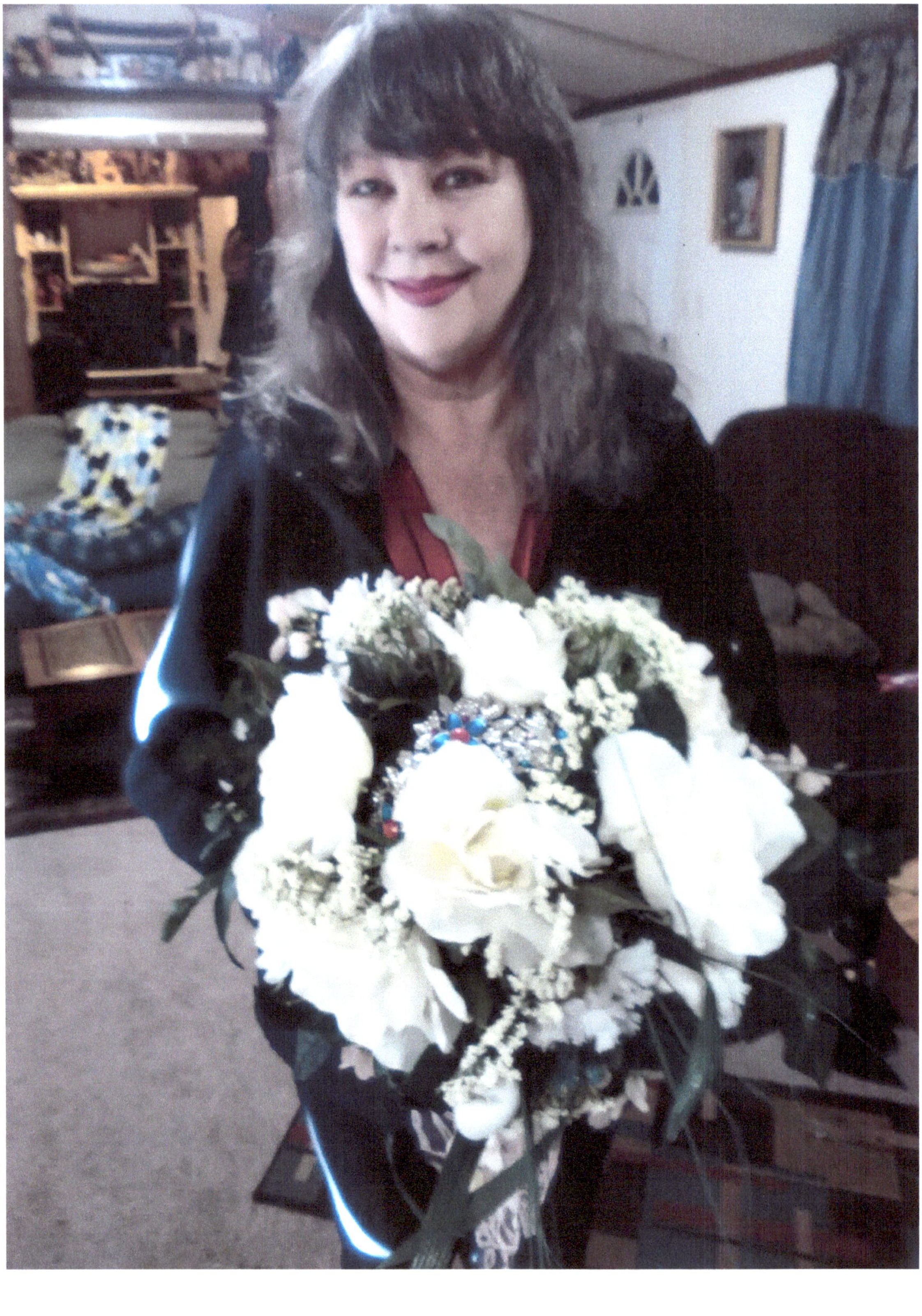

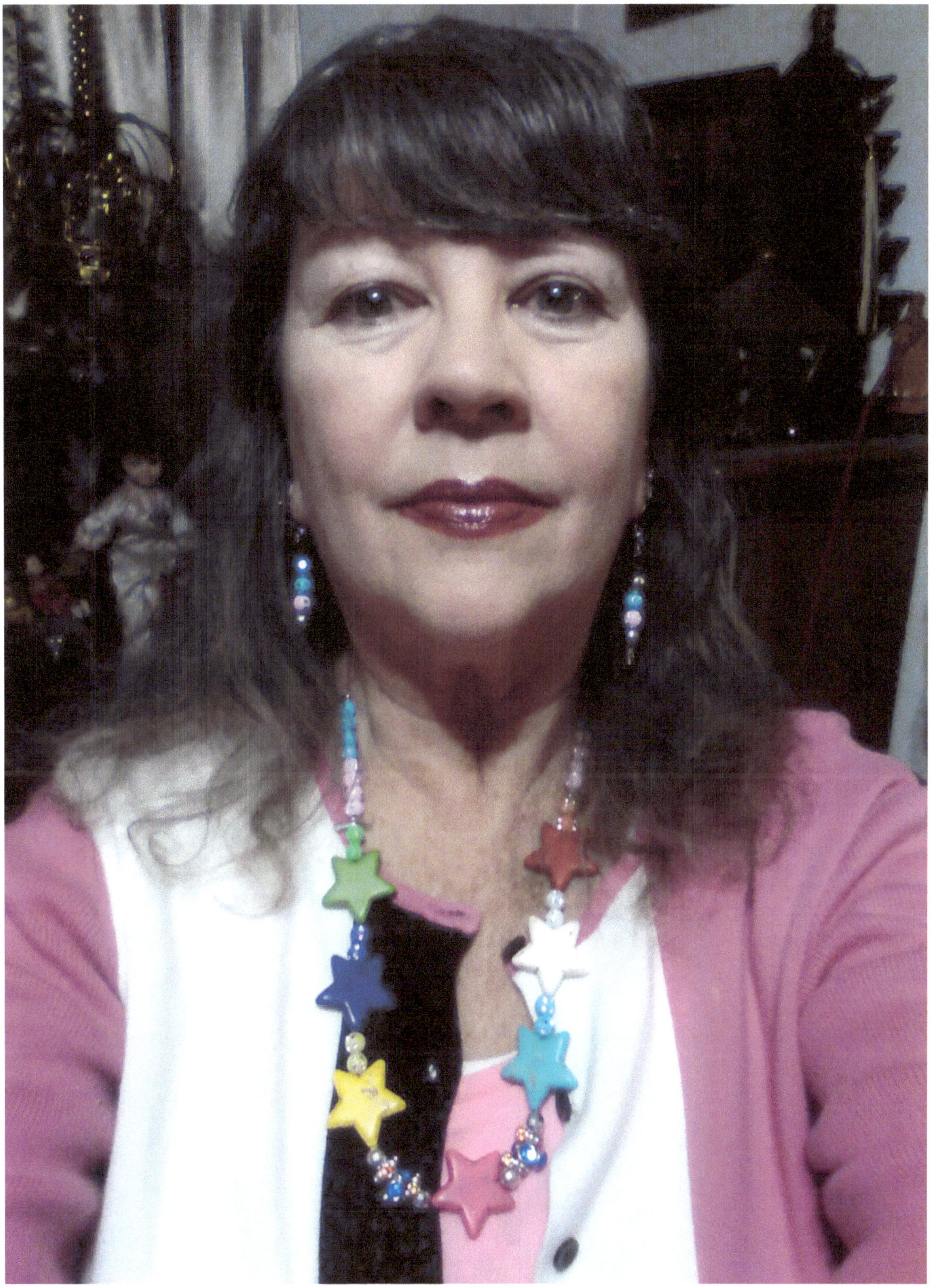

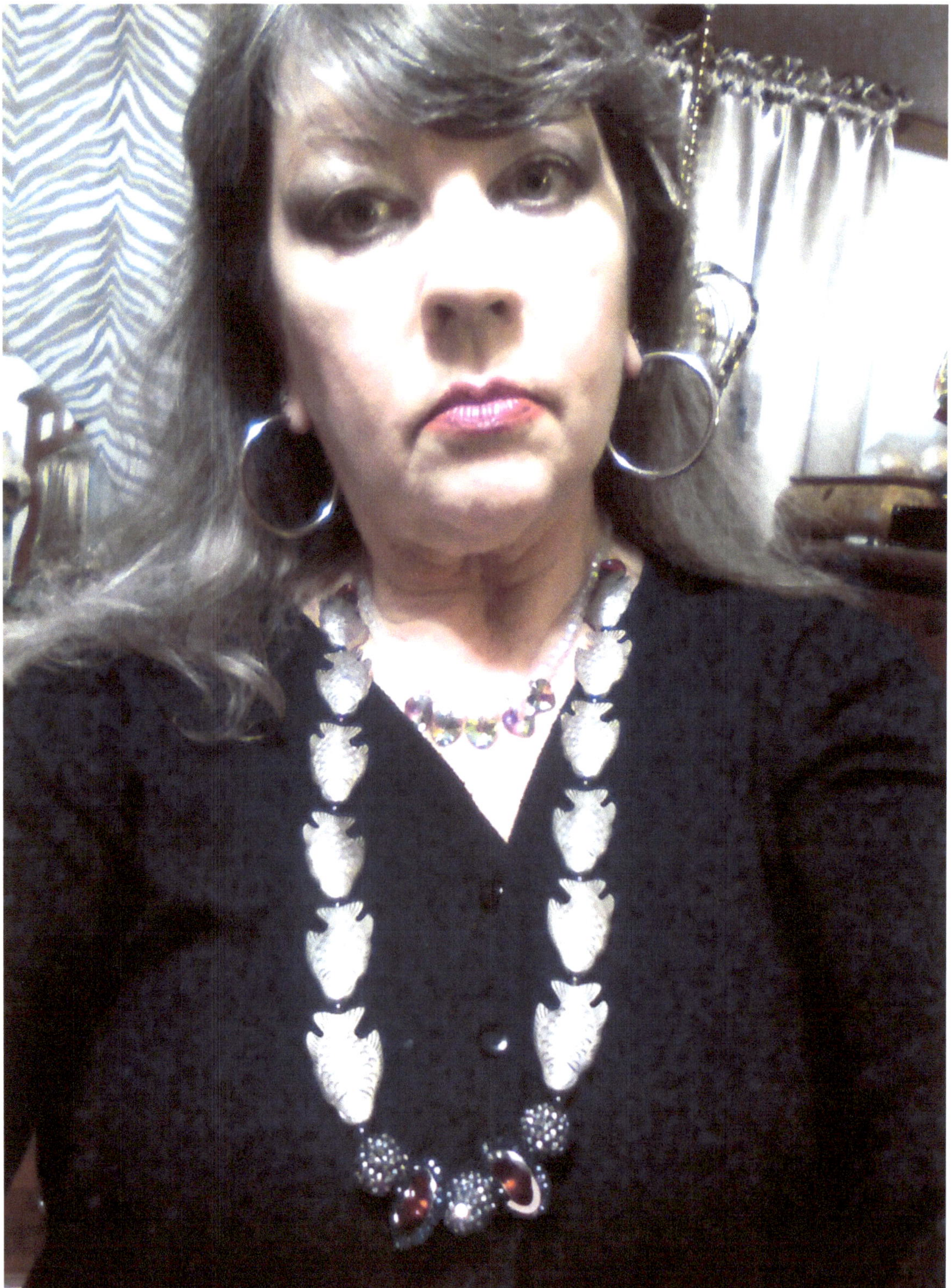

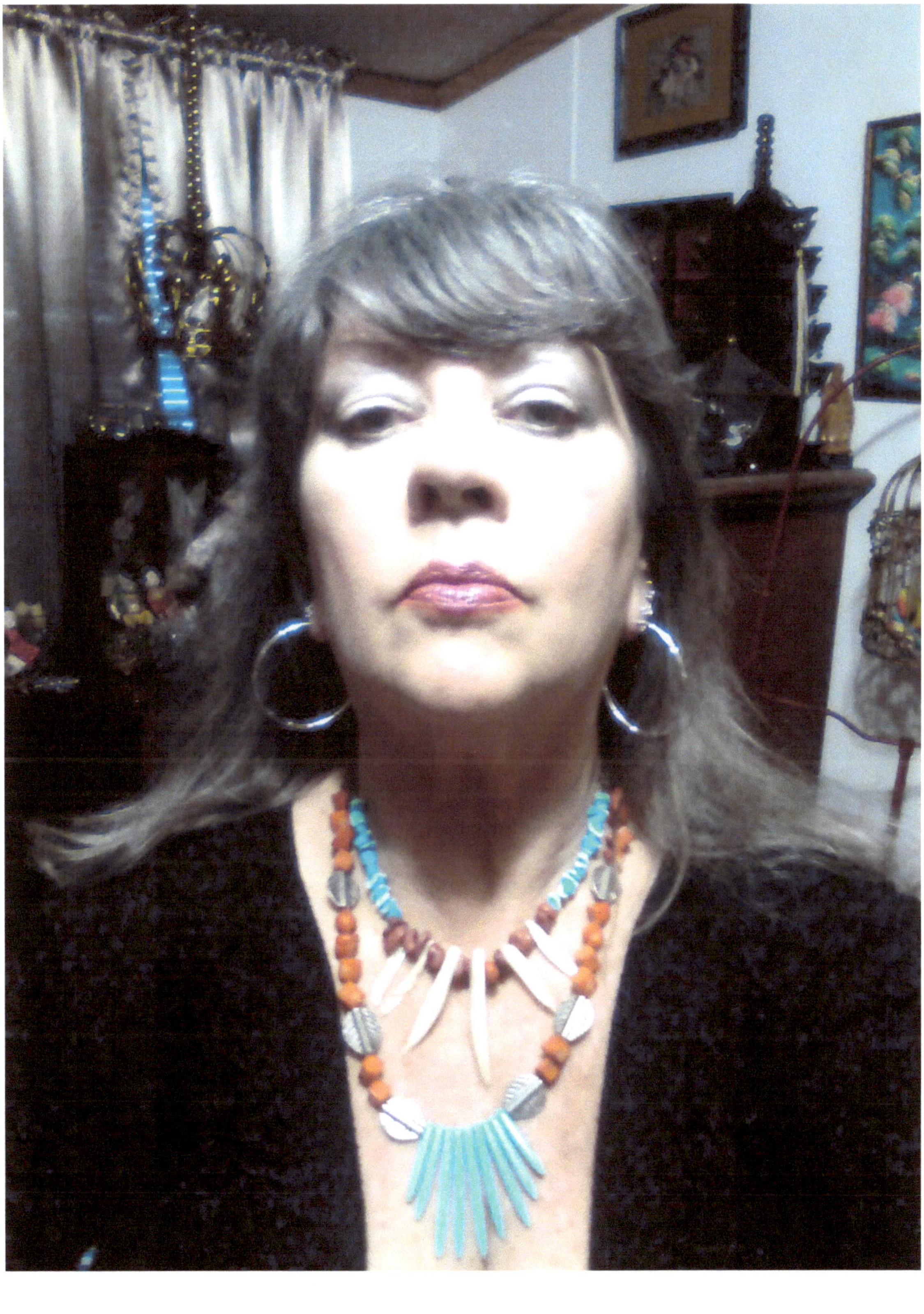

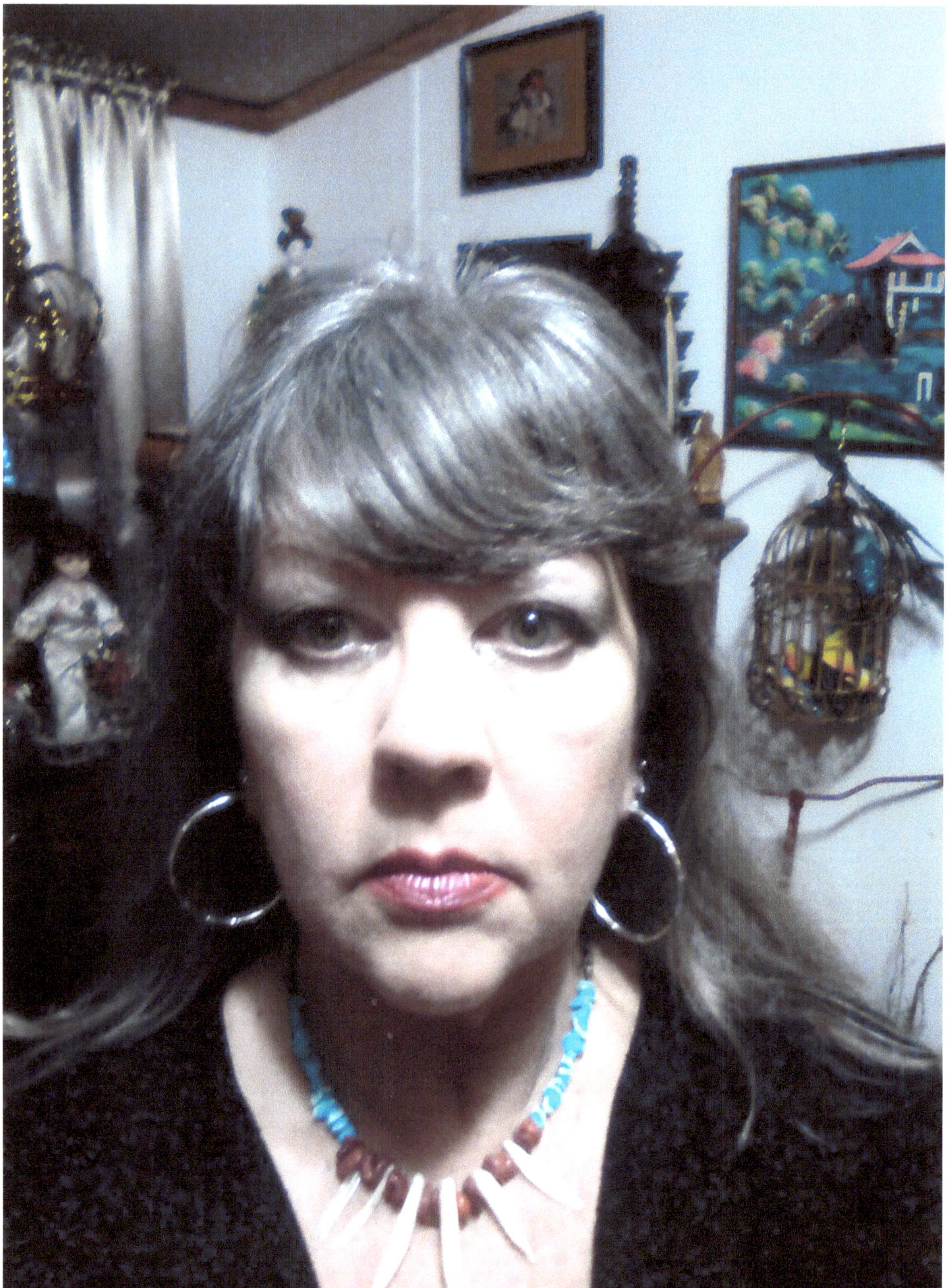

Margaret Of Athens

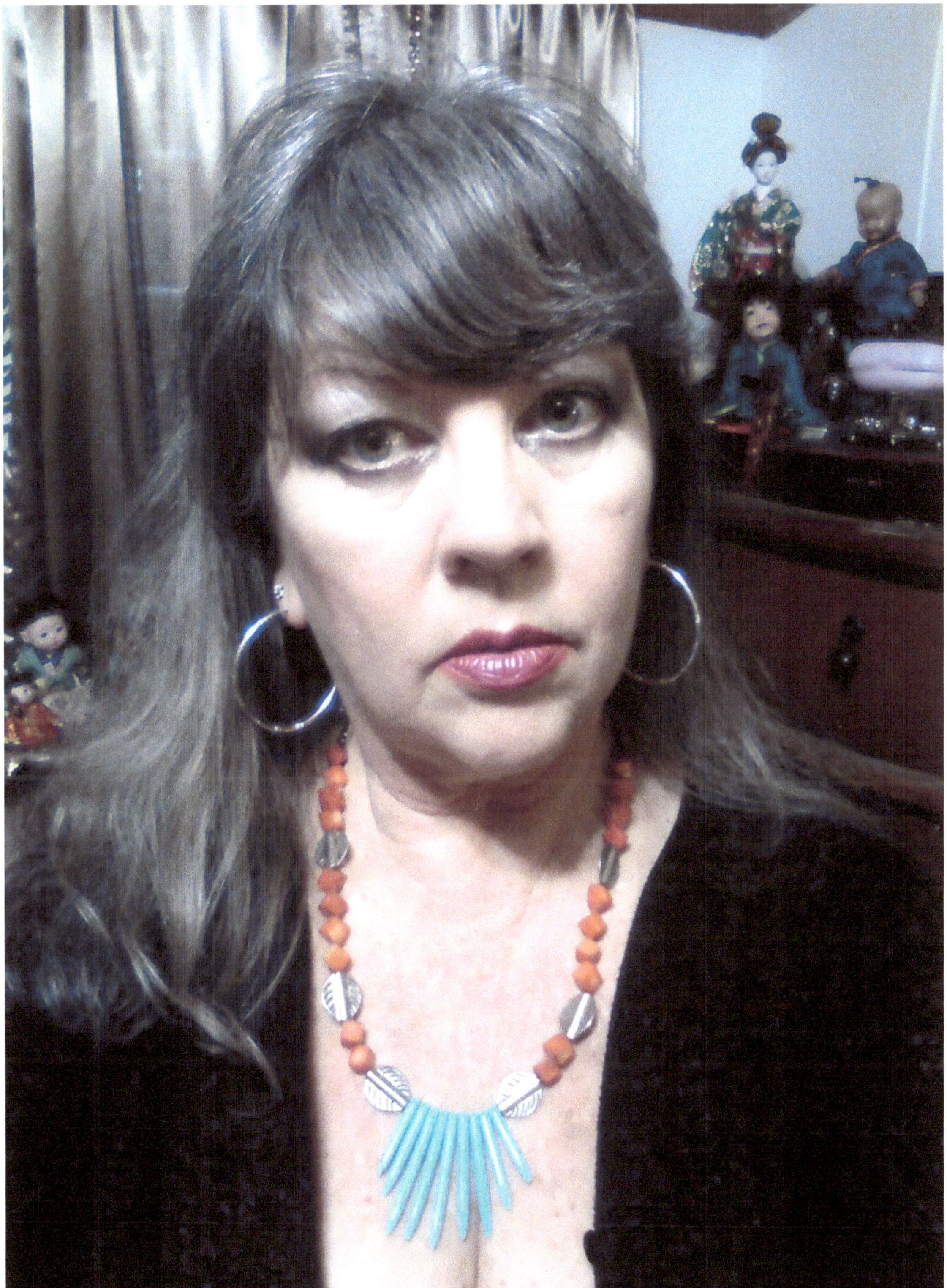

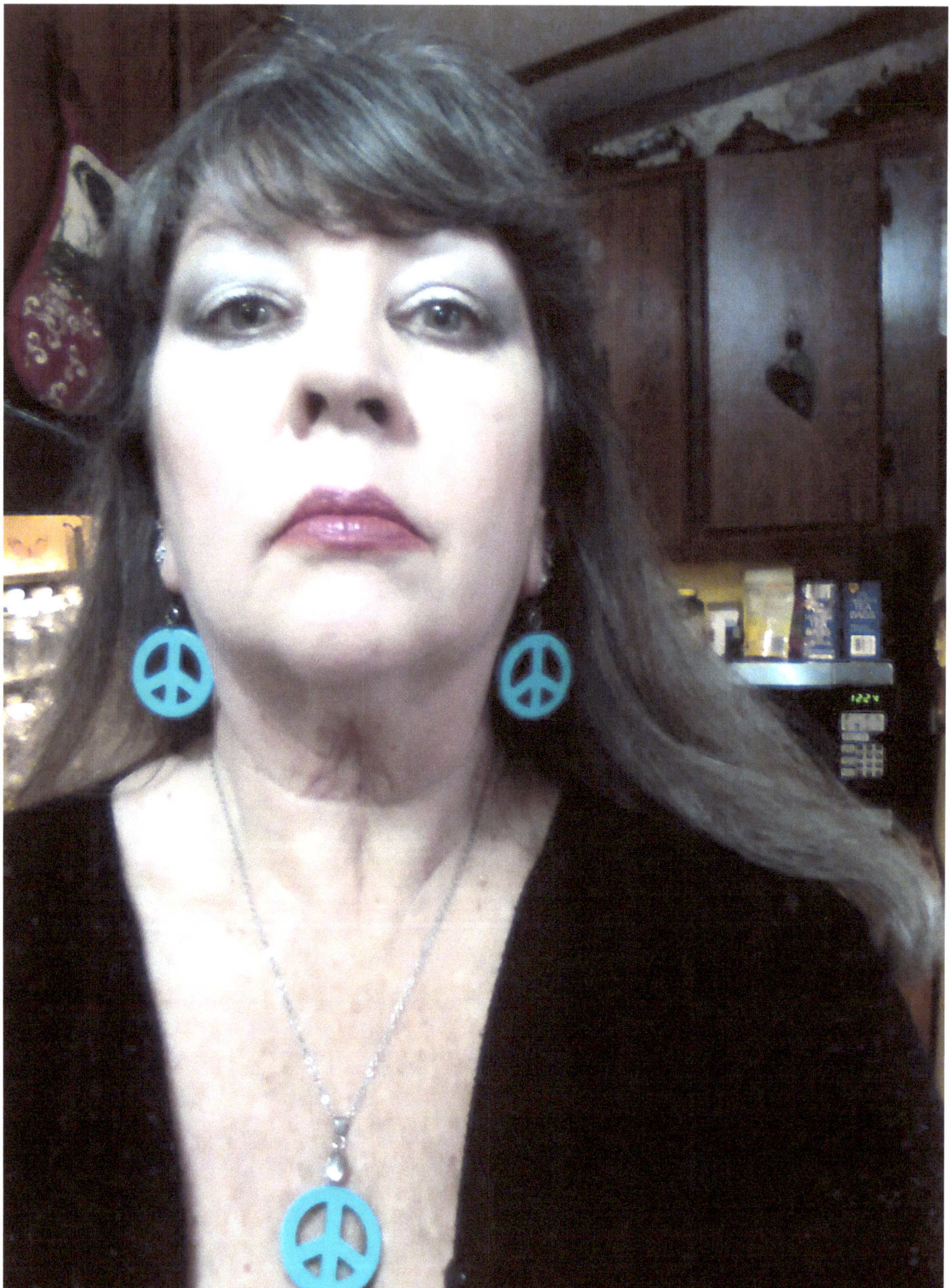

Margaret Of Athens

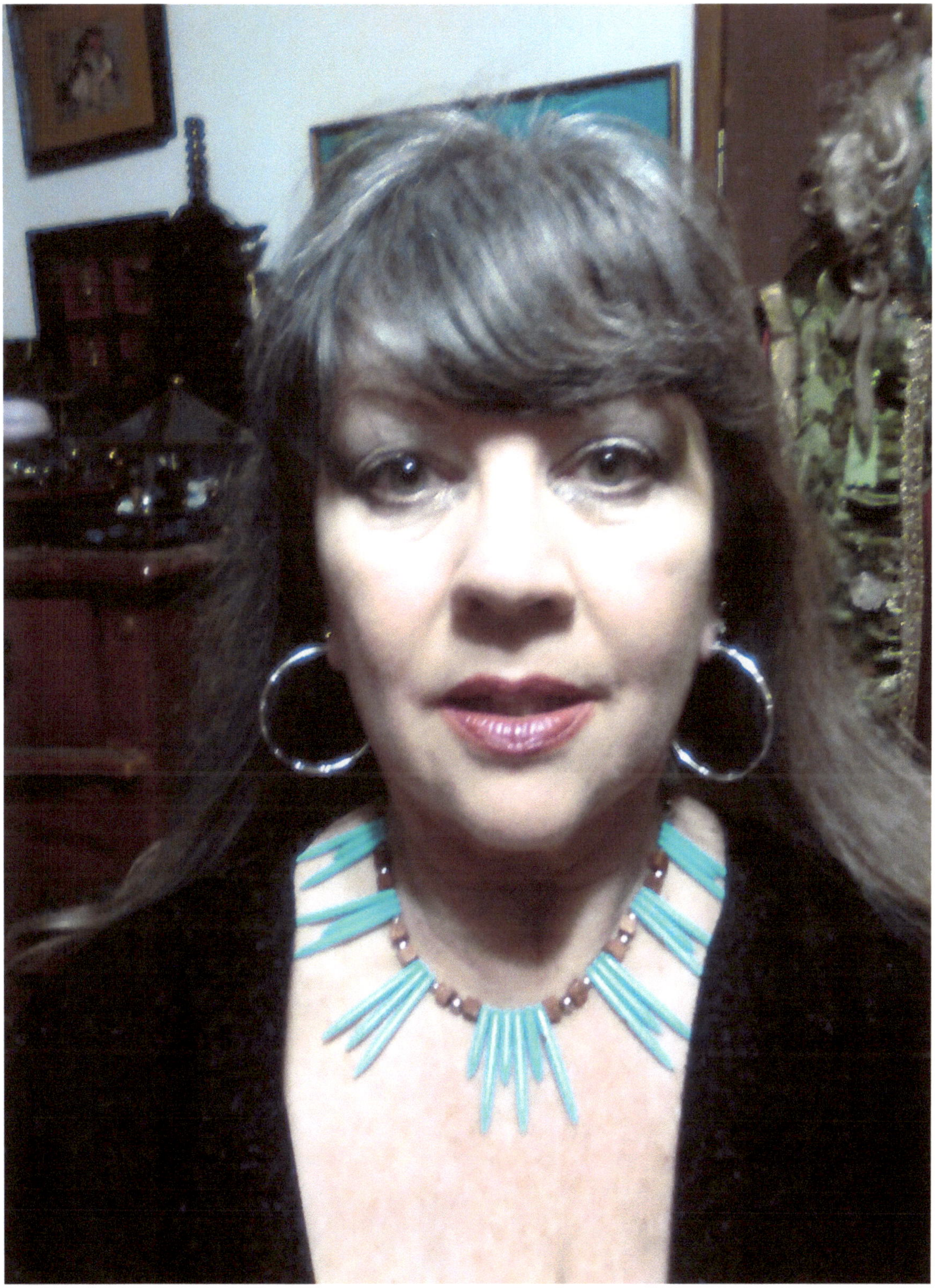

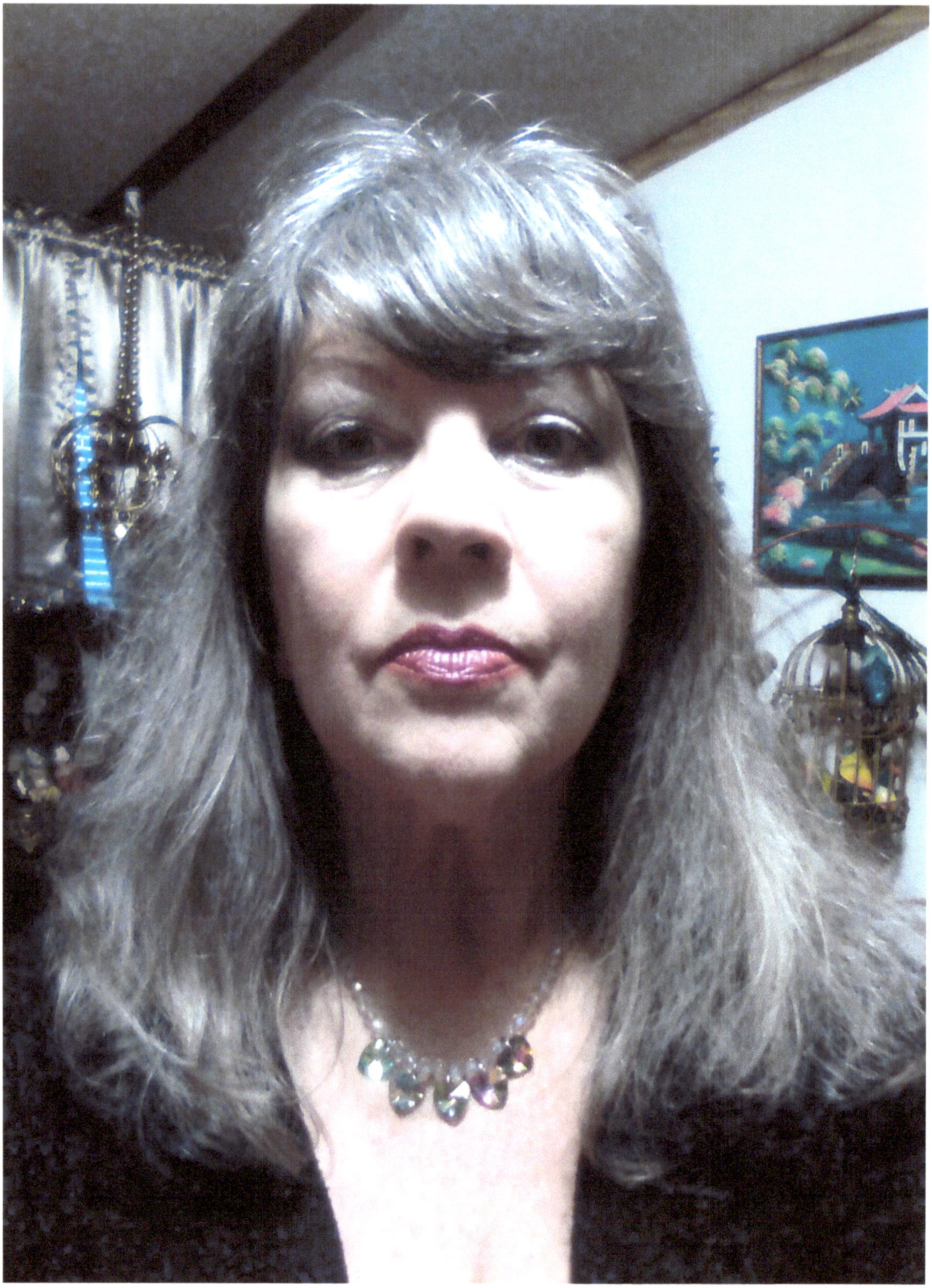

Margaret Of Athens

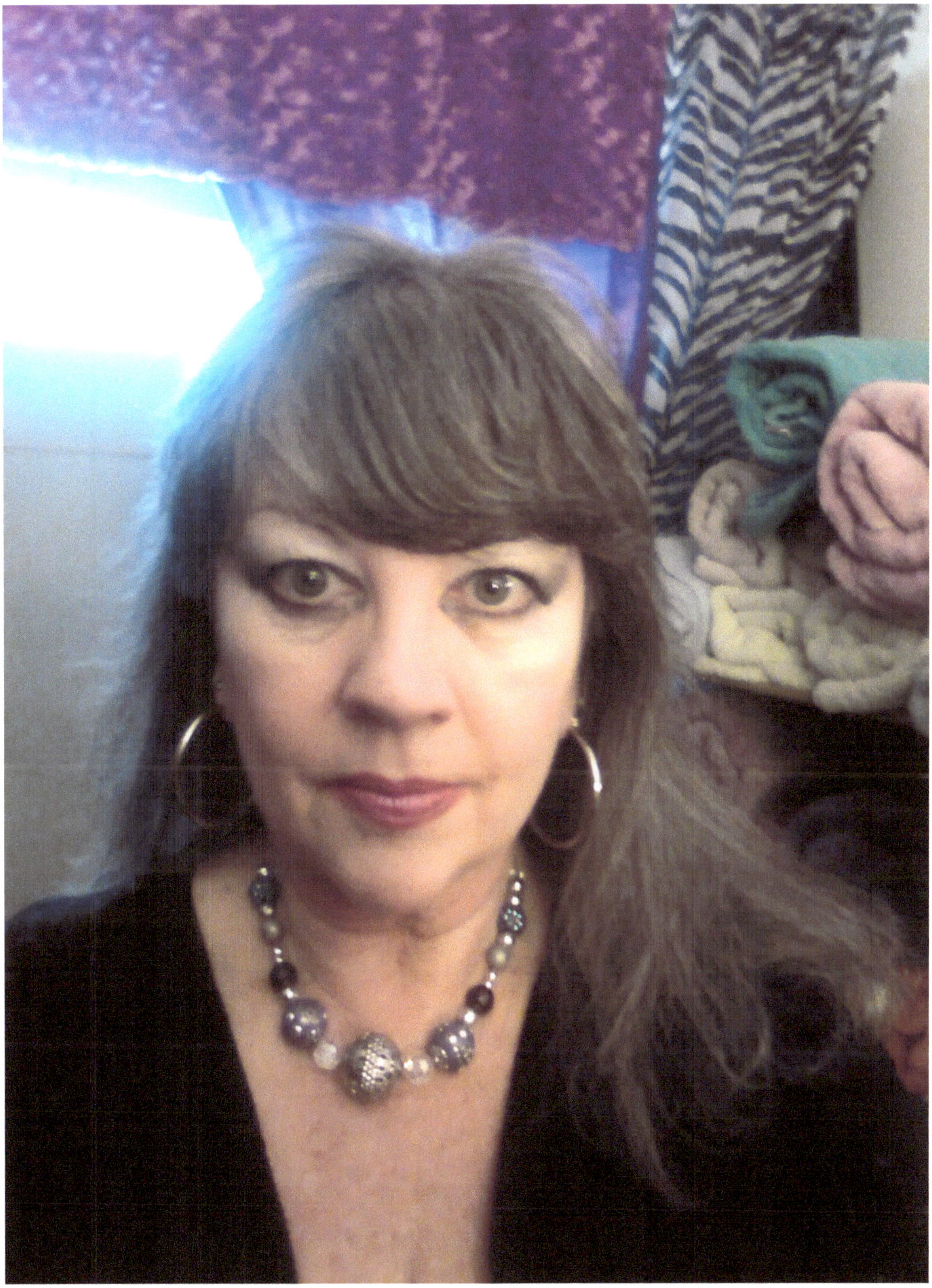

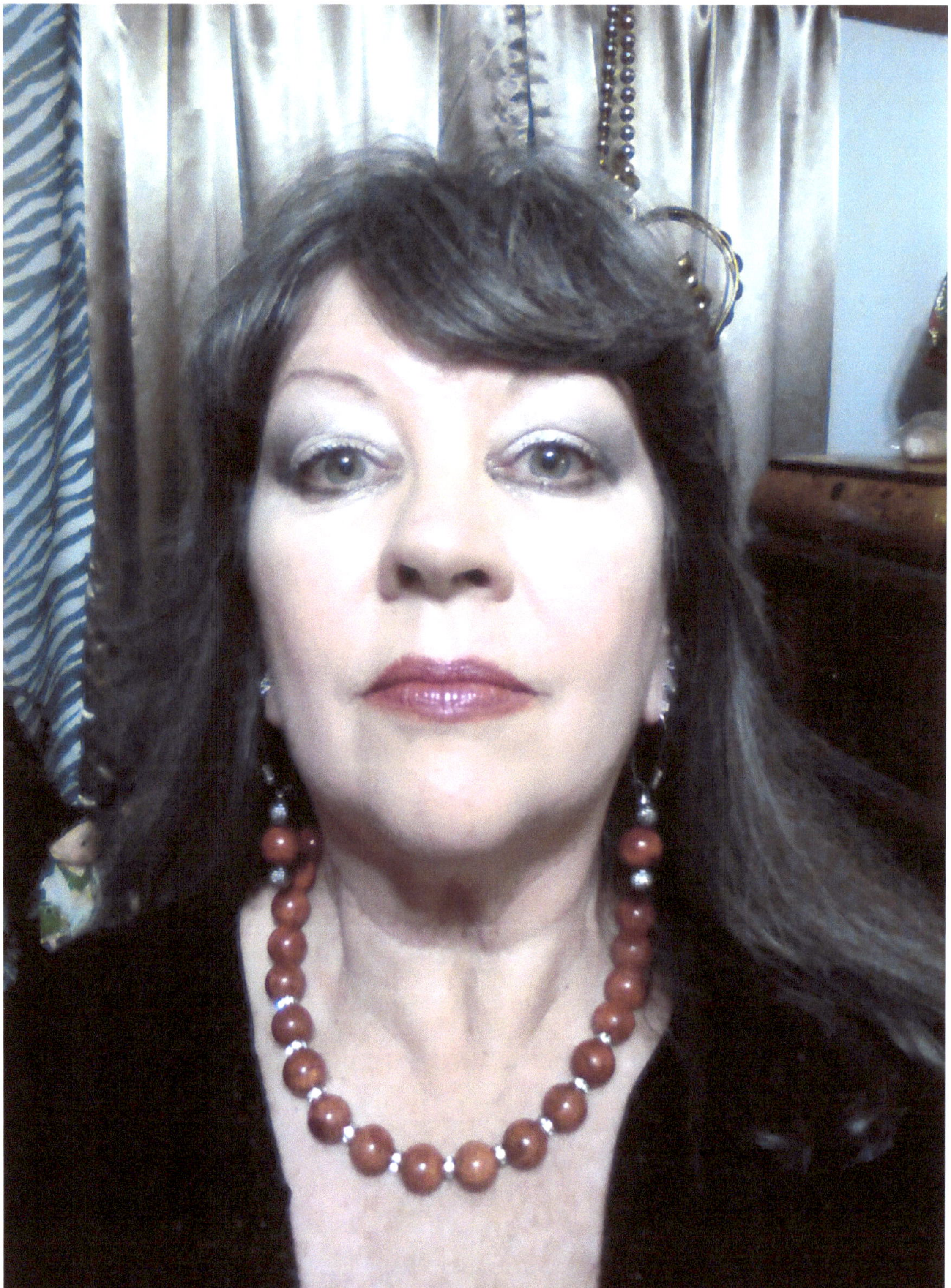

Margaret Of Athens

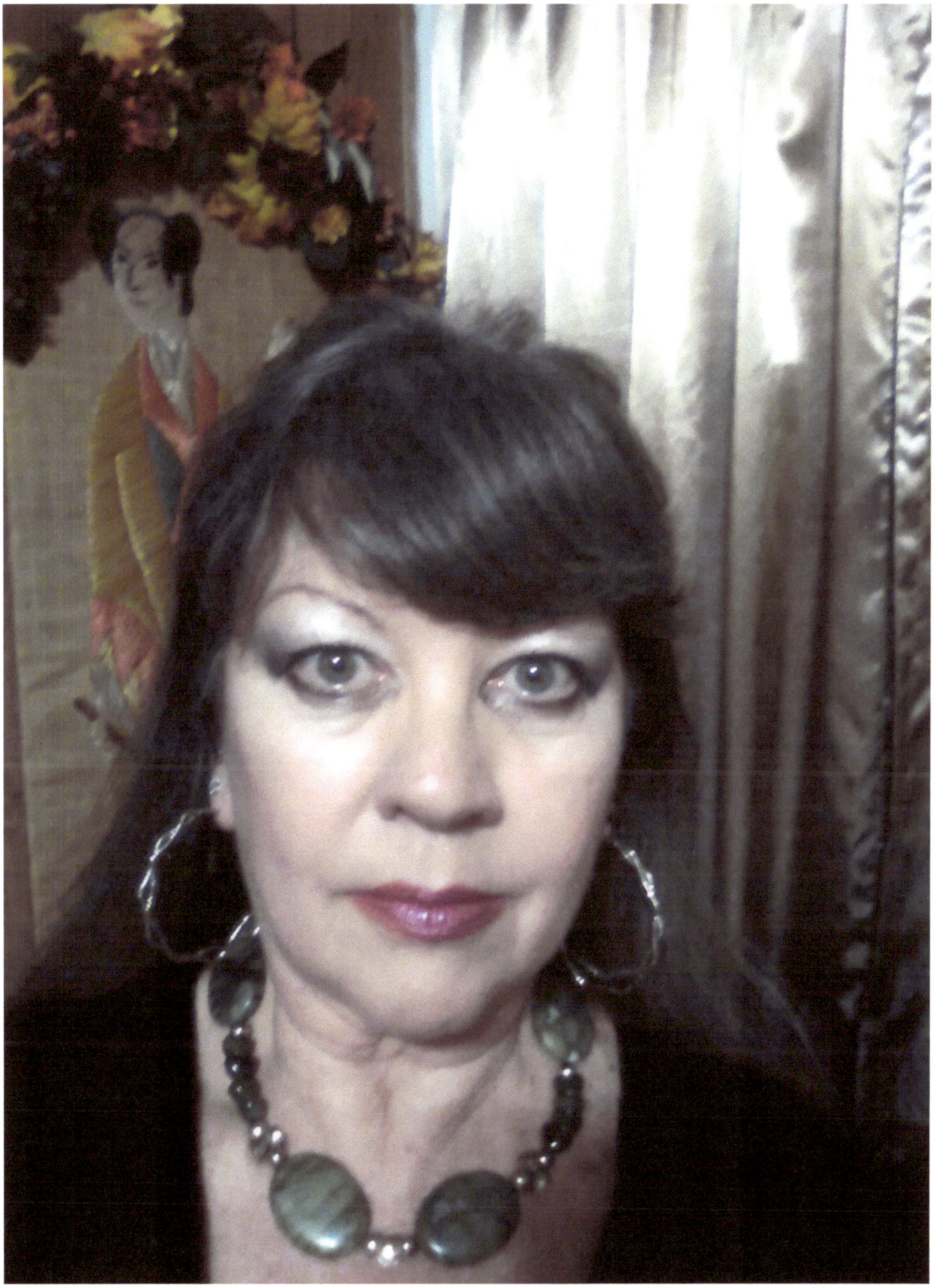

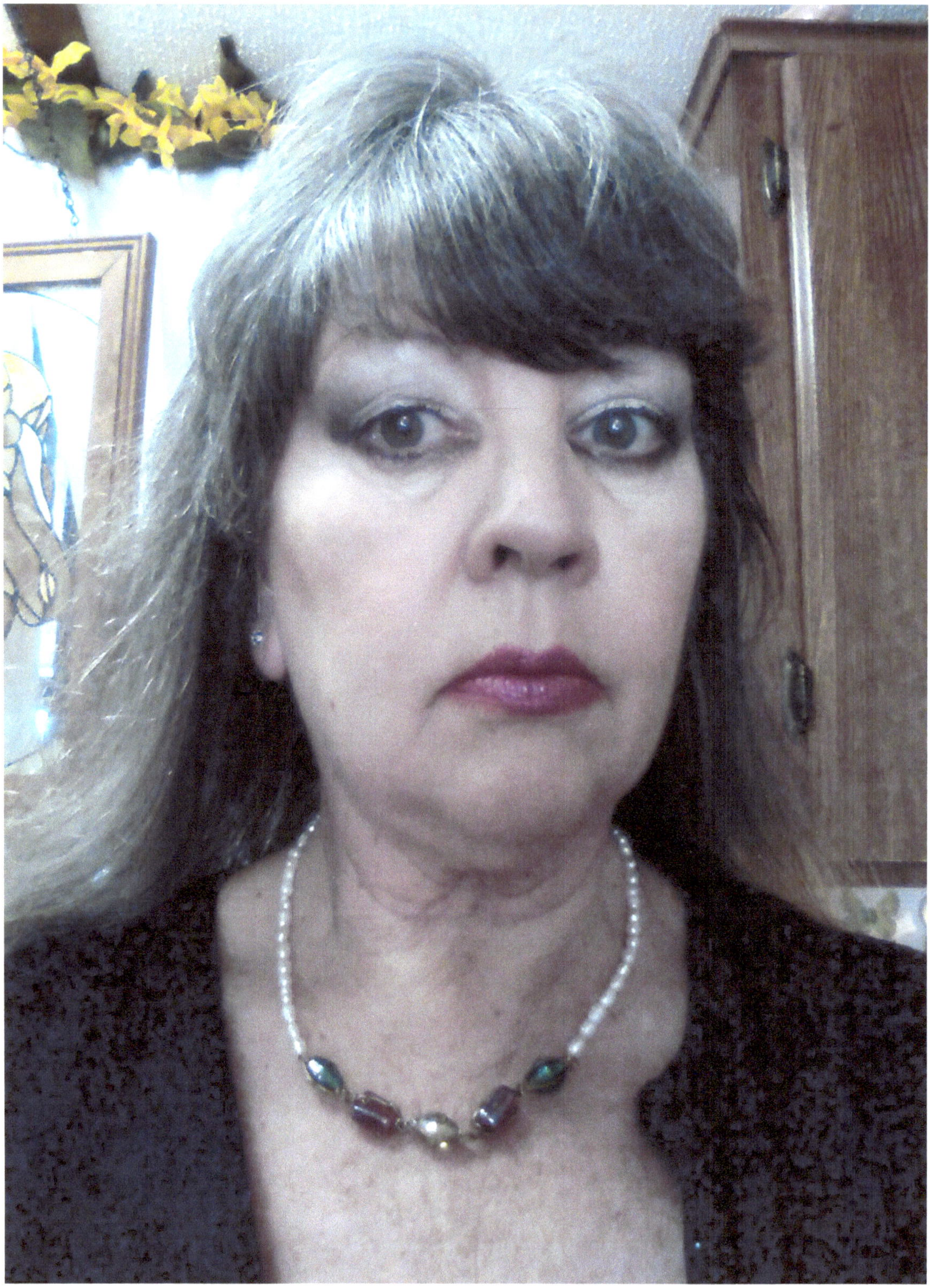

Margaret Of Athens

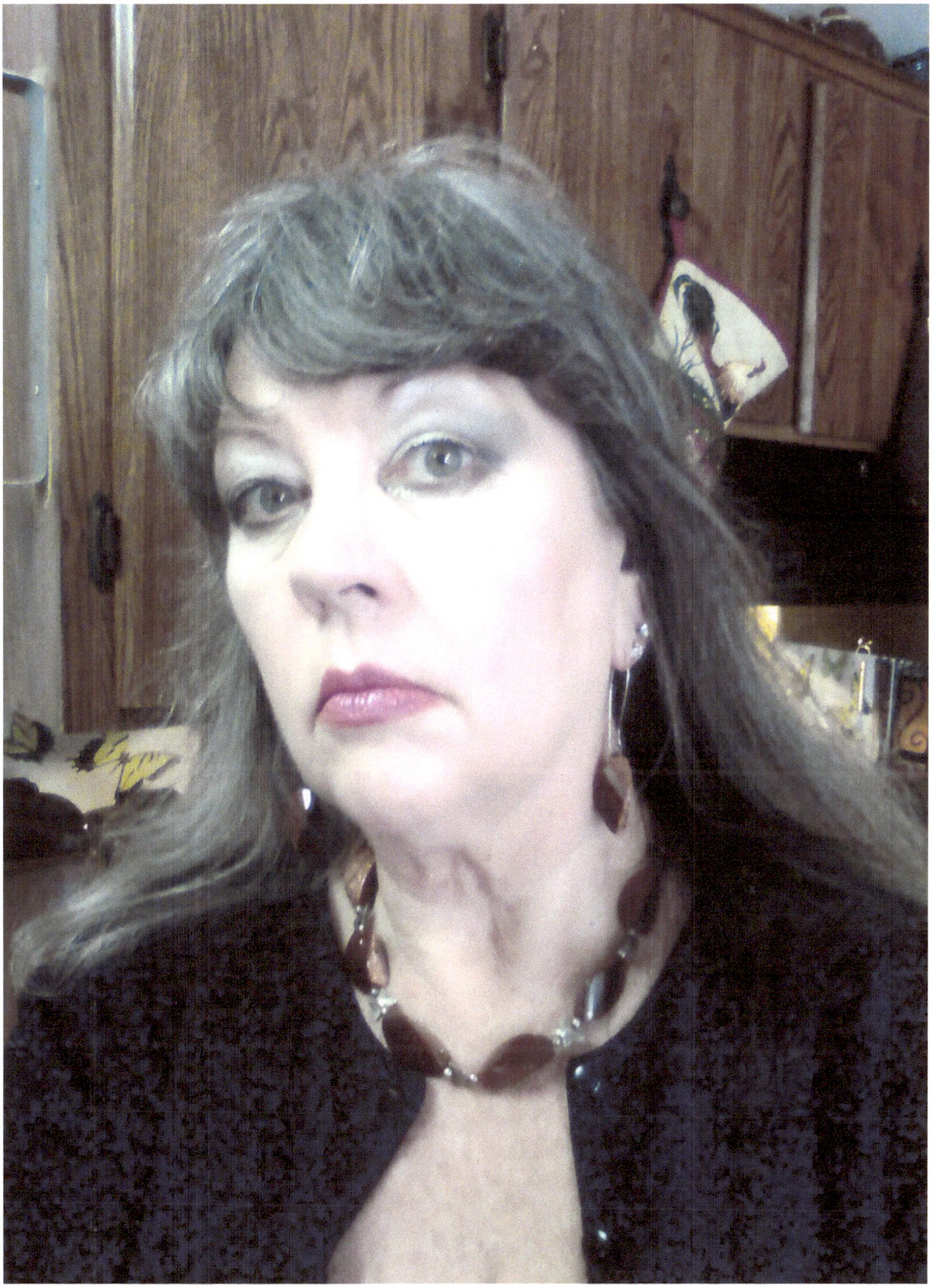

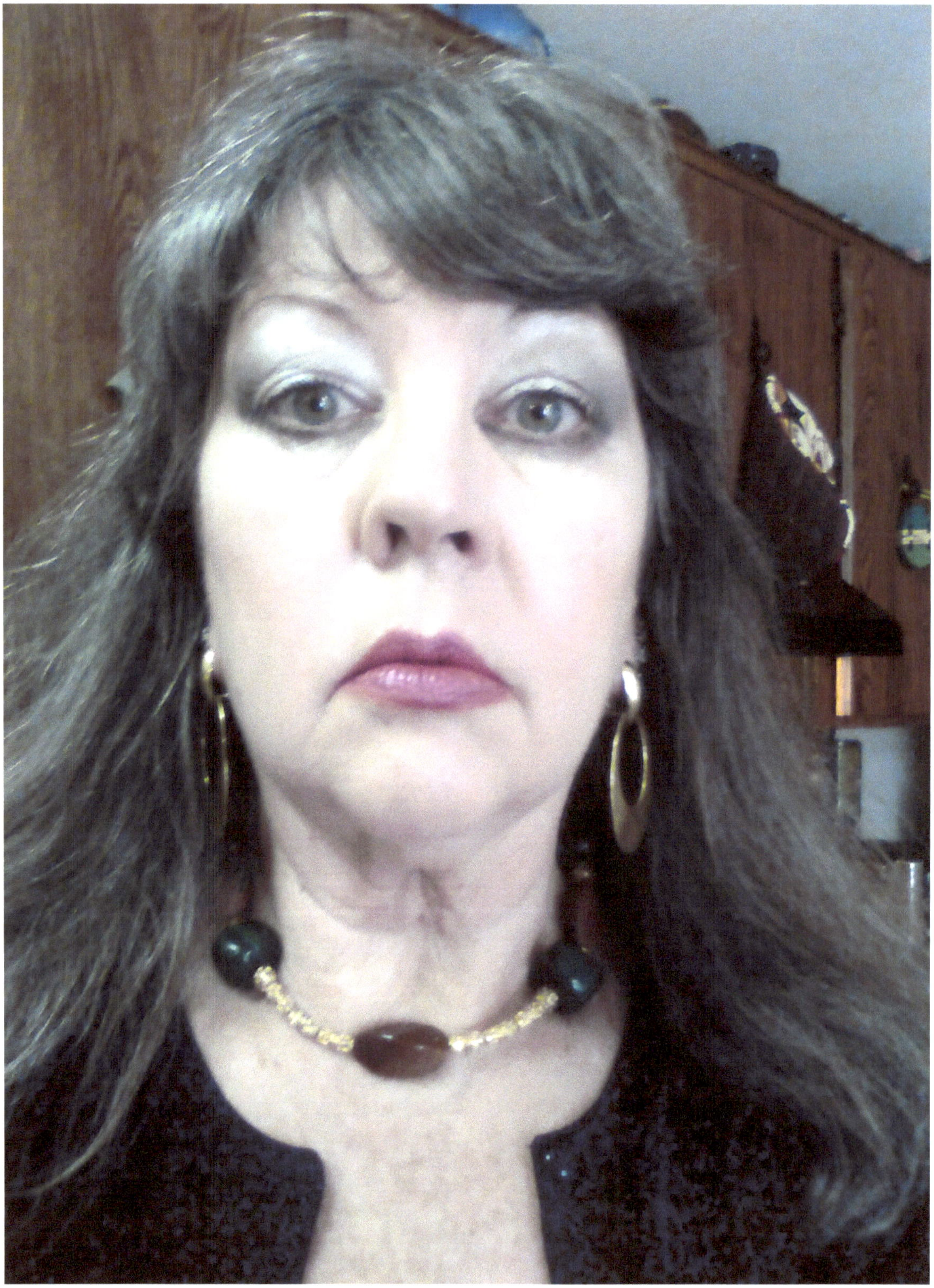

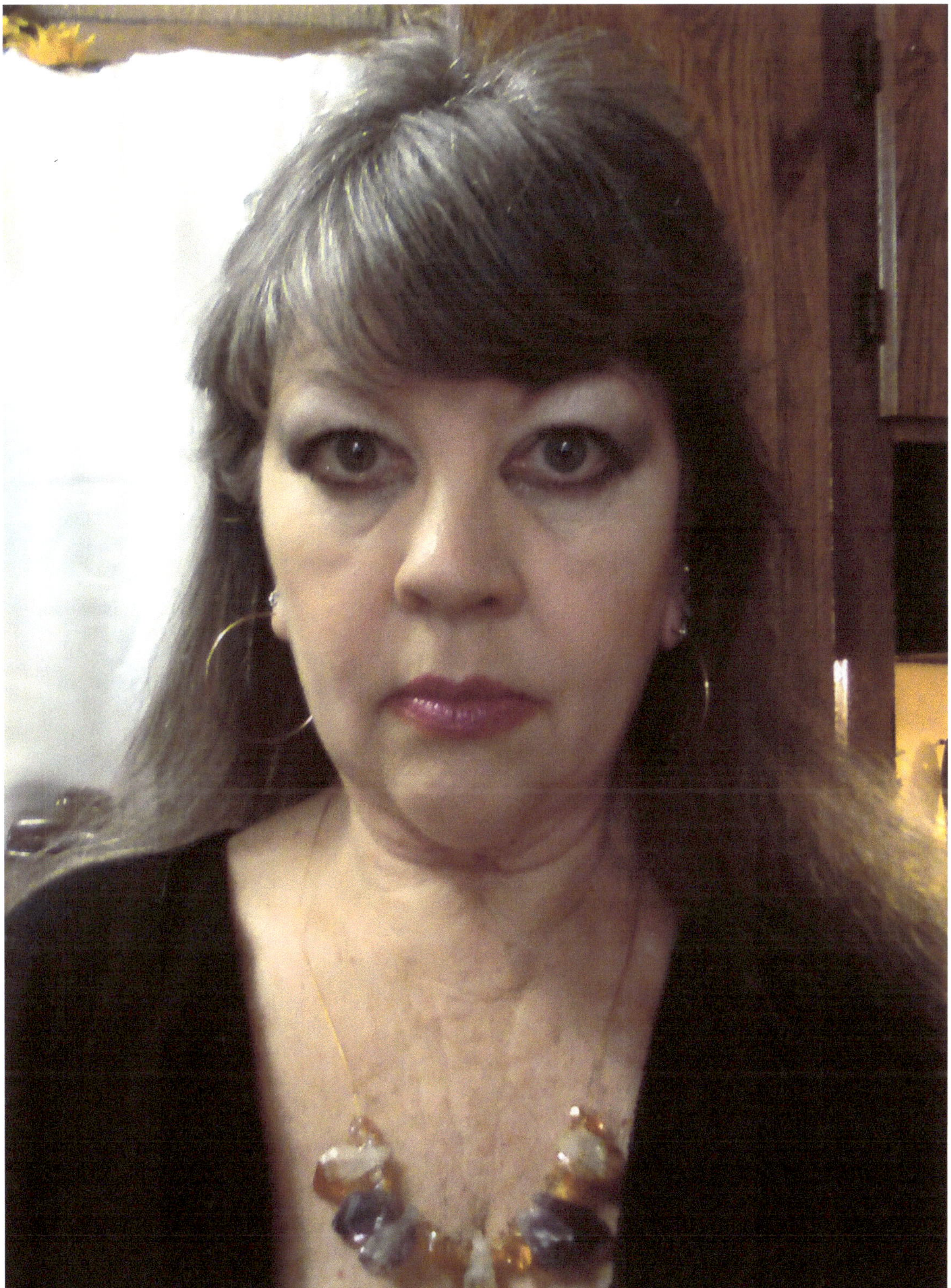

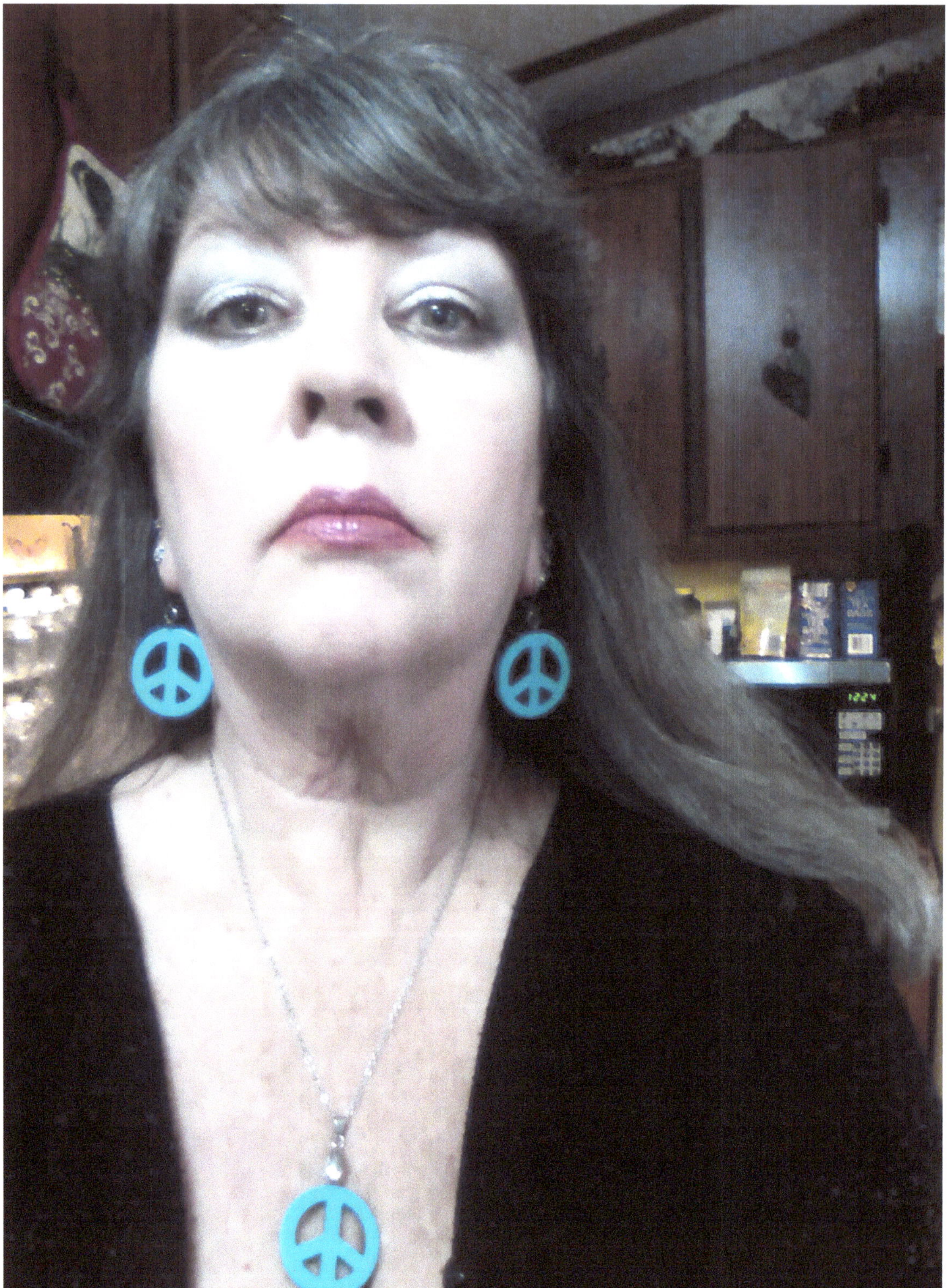

Margaret Of Athens

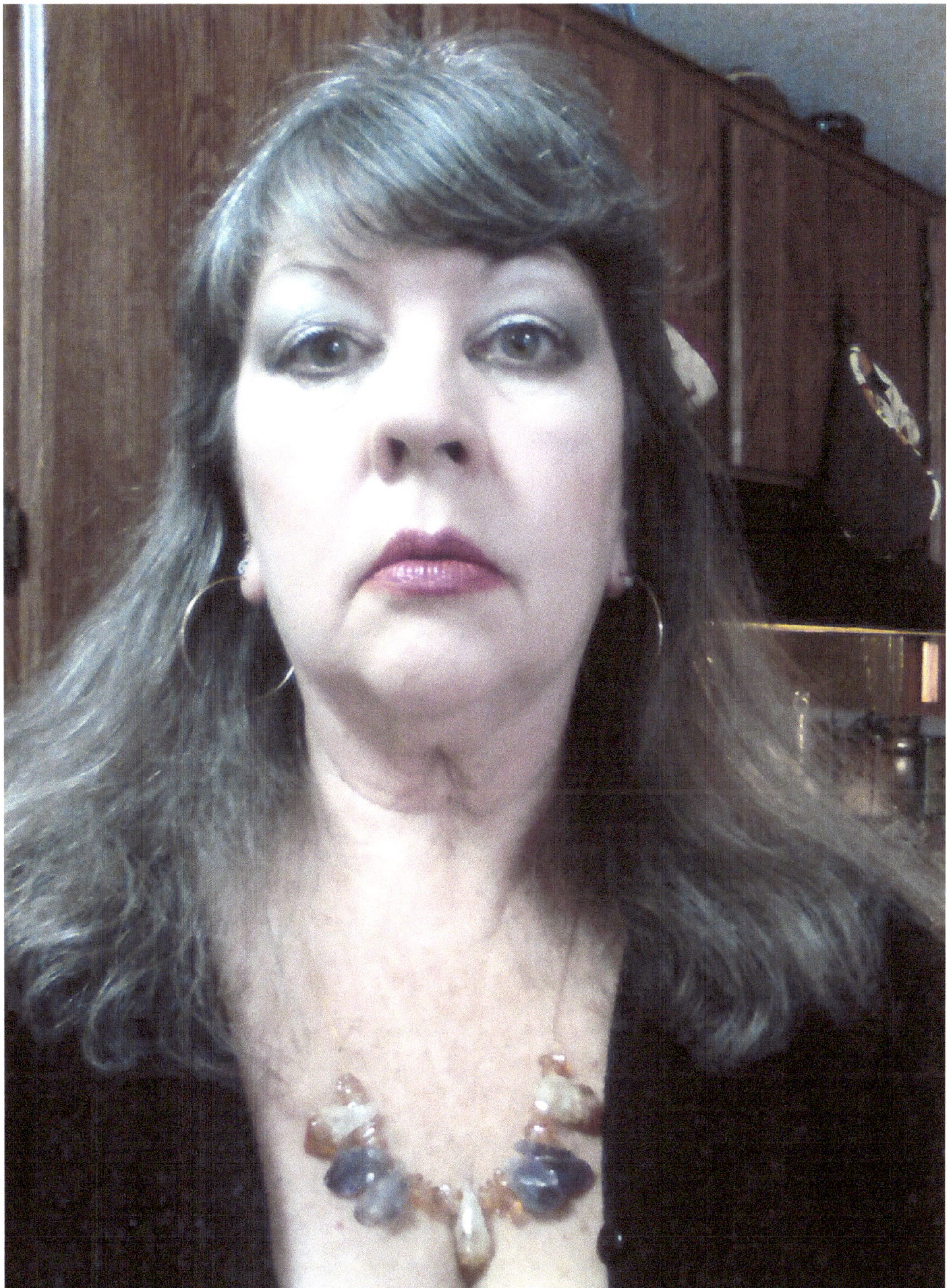

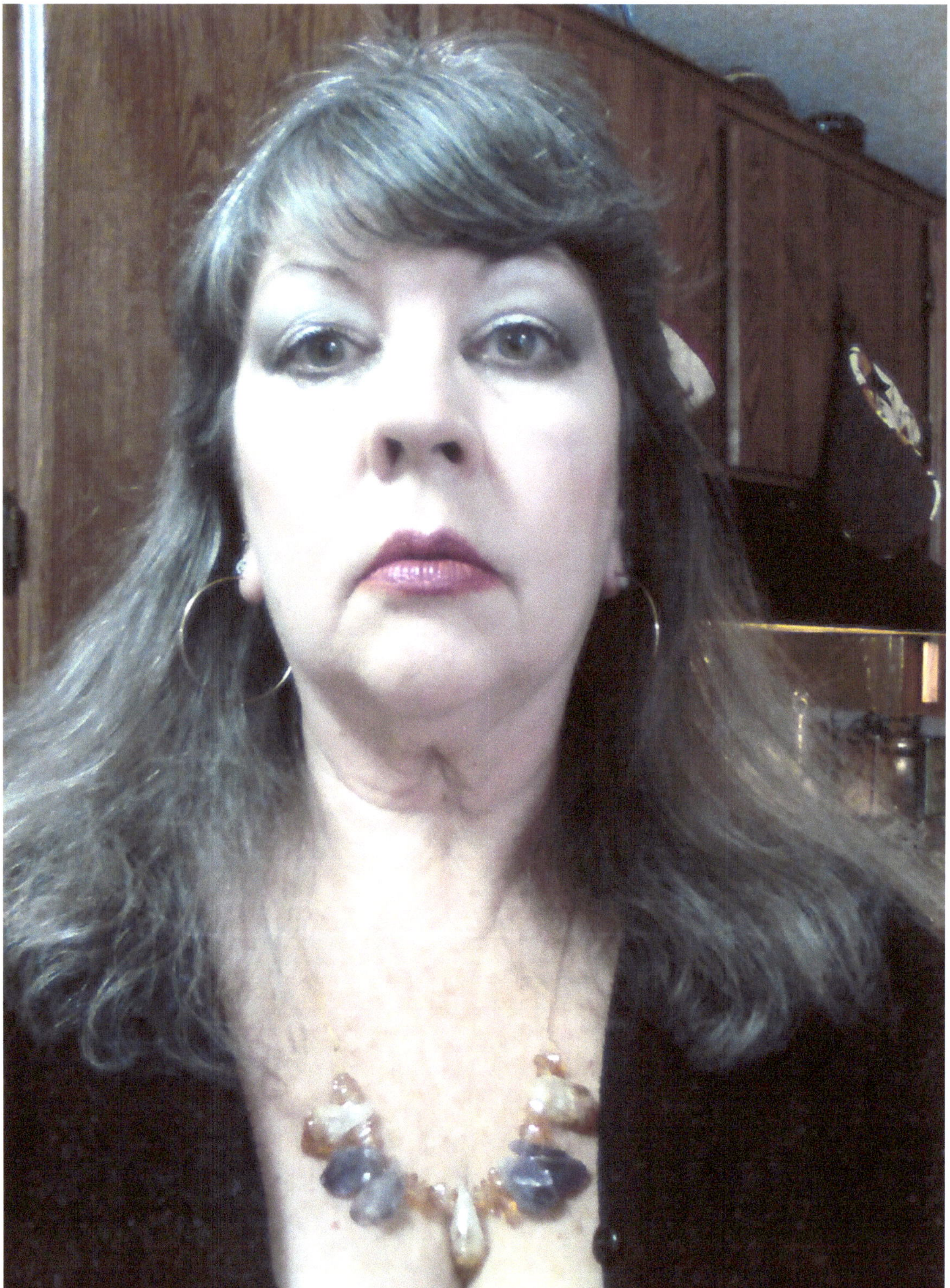

Margaret Of Athens

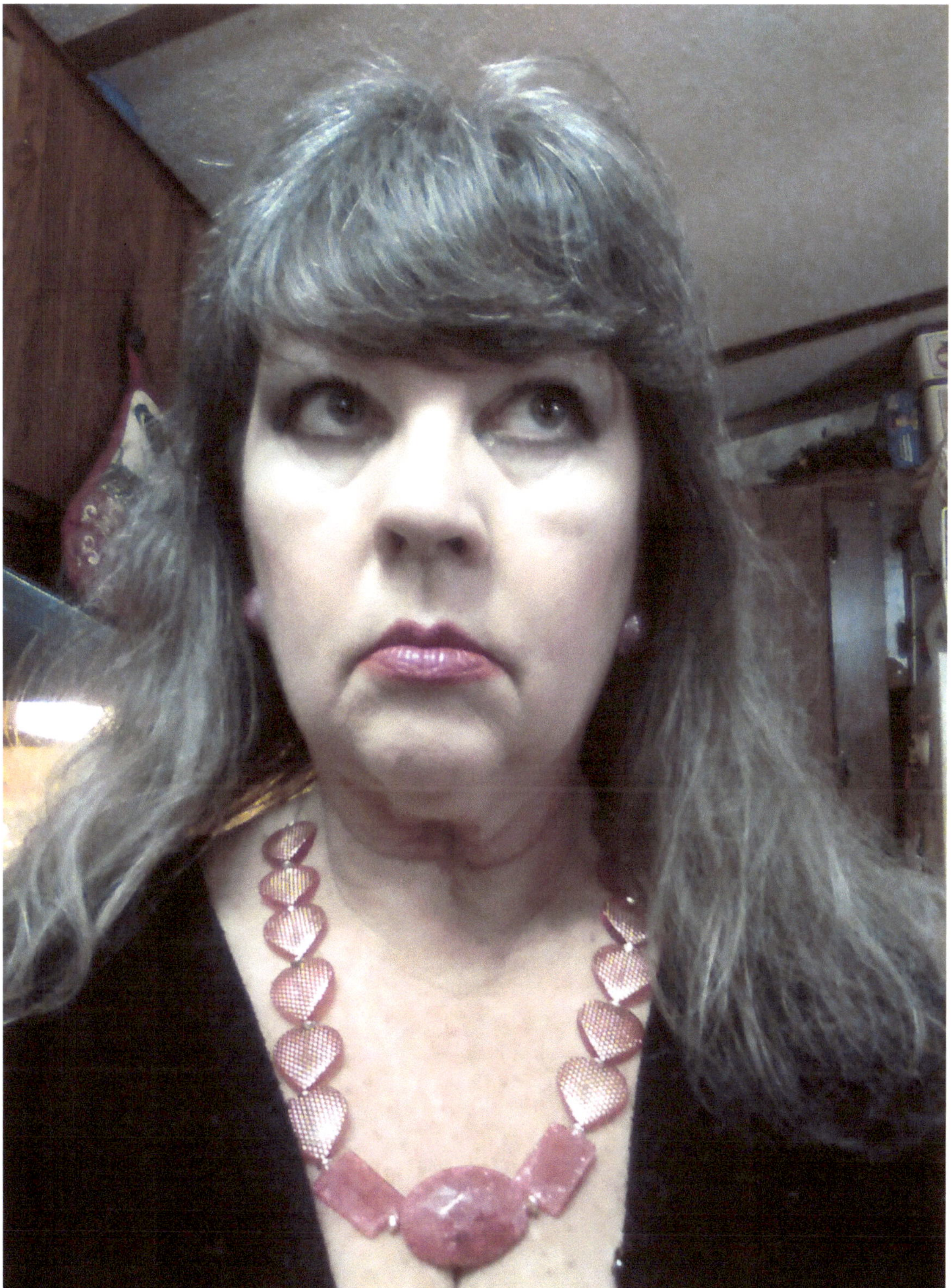

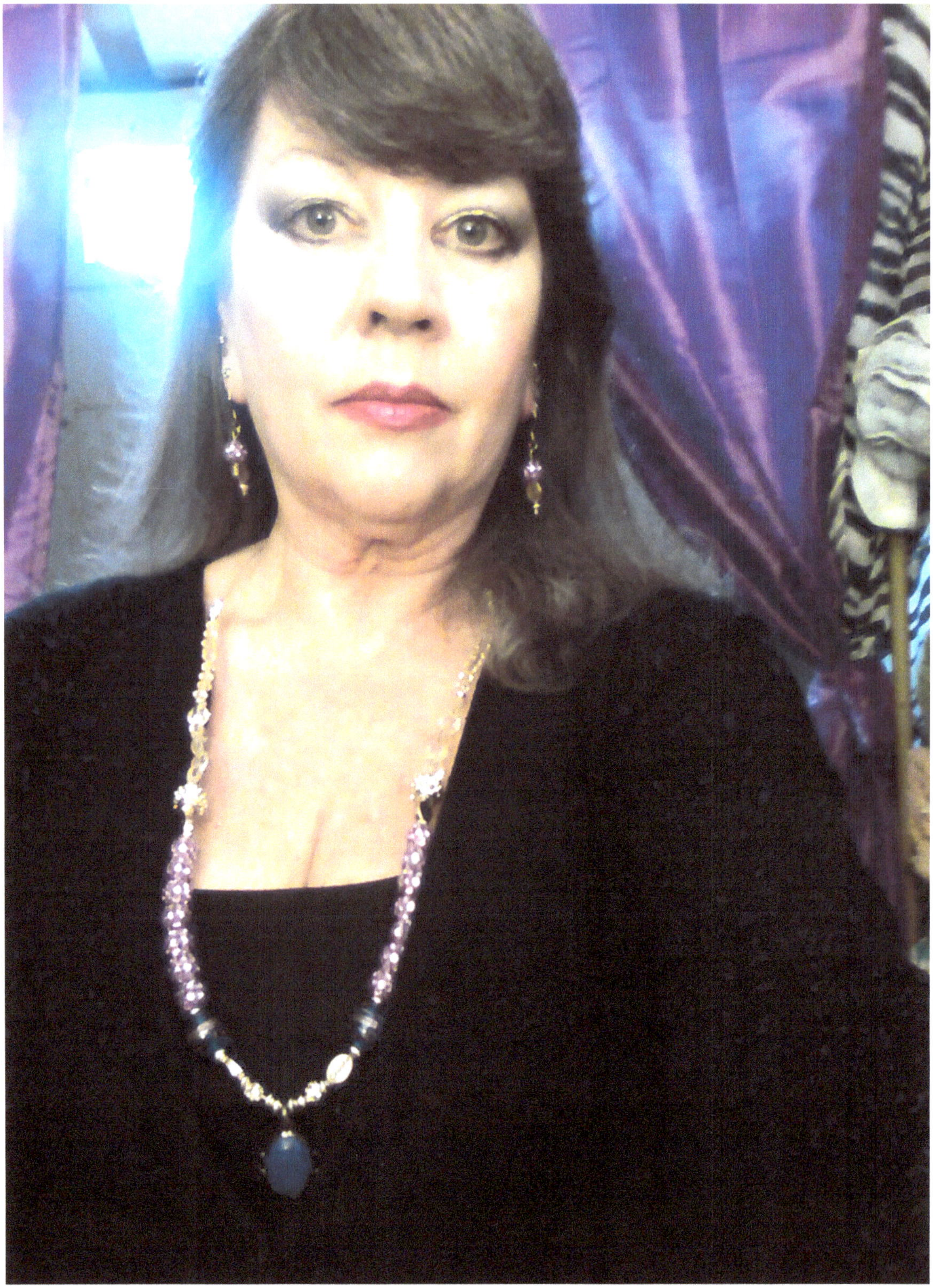

Margaret Of Athens

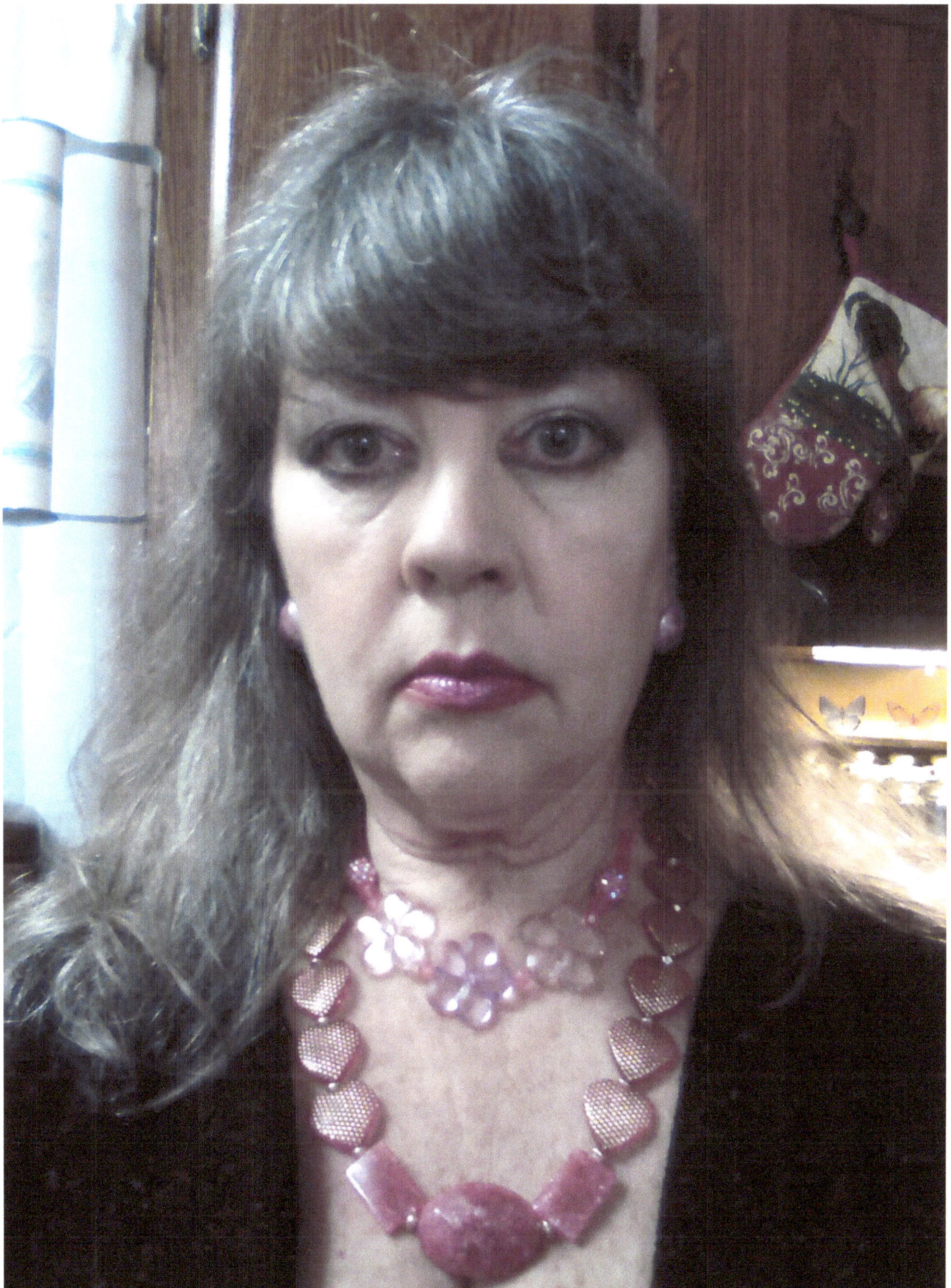

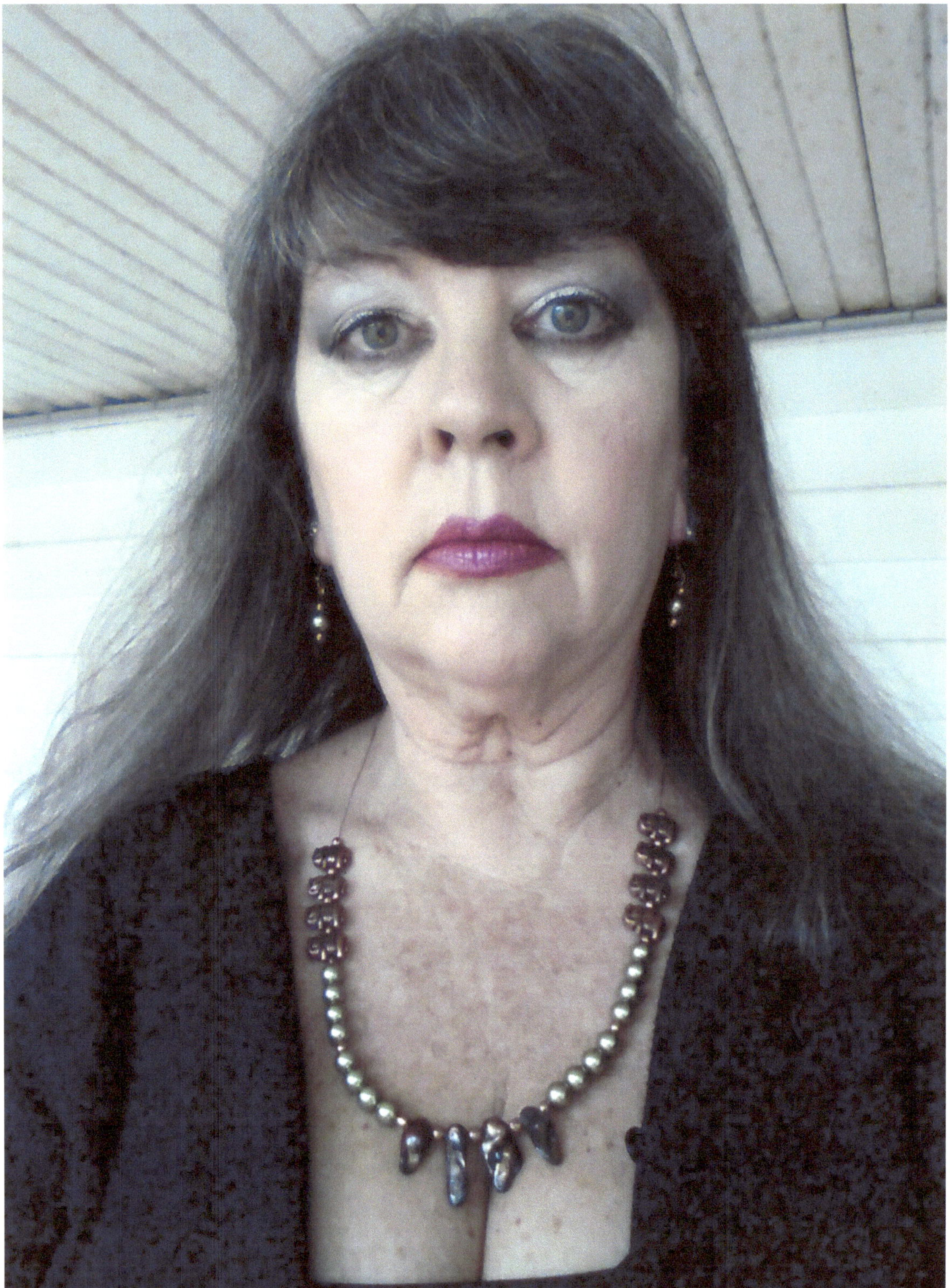

Margaret Of Athens

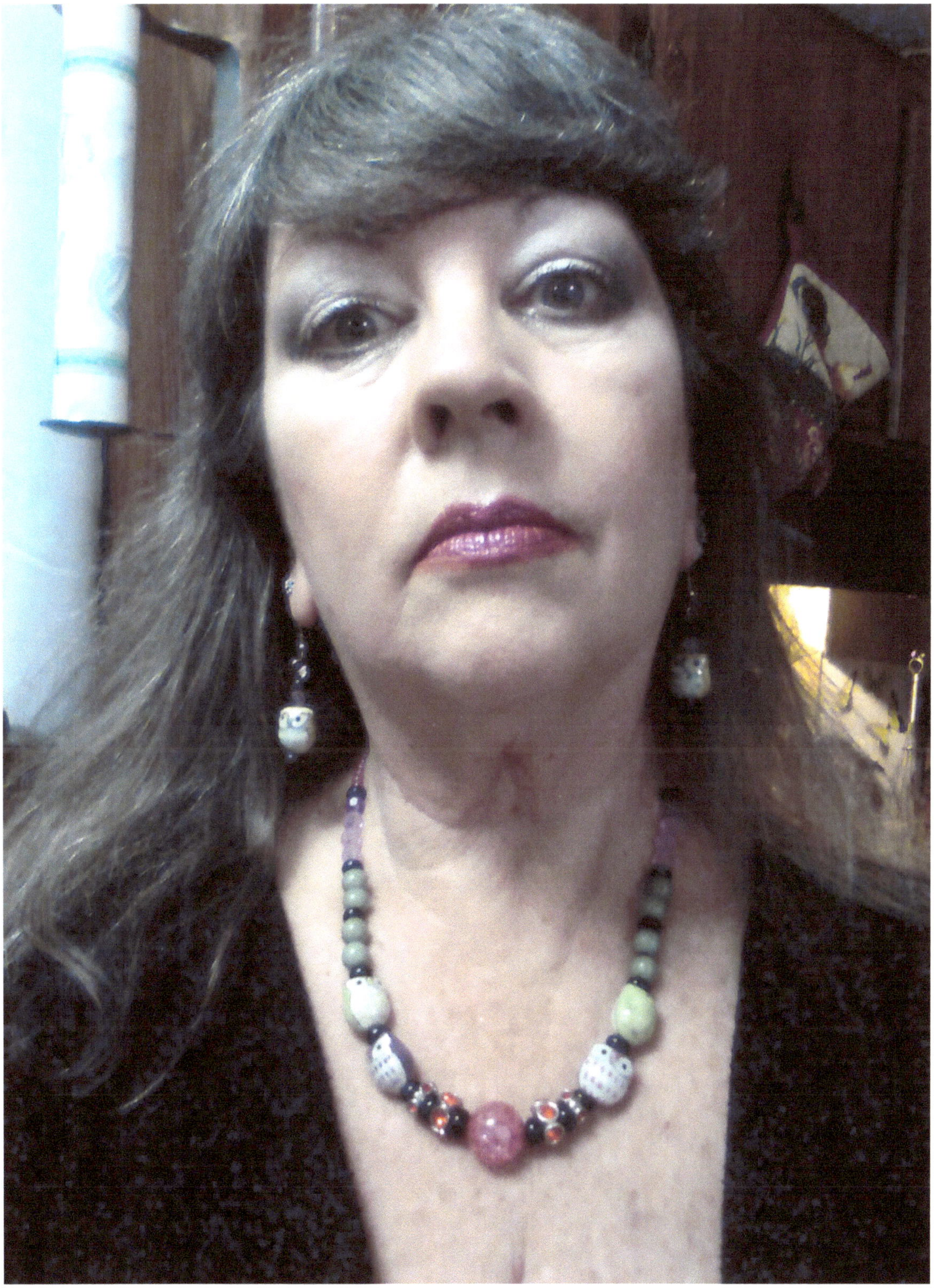

www.ingramcontent.com/pod-product-compliance
Lightning Source LLC
Chambersburg PA
CBHW050413180526
45159CB00005B/2258
* 9 7 8 1 5 1 1 4 1 3 1 2 1 *